Fiction an

MW00781578

This challenging study places fiction squarely at the center of the discussion of metaphysics. Philosophers have traditionally treated fiction as involving a set of narrow problems in logic or the philosophy of language. By contrast Amie Thomasson argues that fiction has far-reaching implications for central problems of metaphysics.

The book develops an "artifactual" theory of fiction, whereby fictional characters are abstract artifacts as ordinary as laws or symphonies or works of literature. The metaphysical consequences of recognizing abstract artifacts include a new set of basic ontological categories, a clearer understanding of the difference between genuine and false parsimony, and a basis for an adequate ontology of the everyday world. By understanding fictional characters we come to understand how other cultural and social objects are established on the basis of the independent physical world and the mental states of human beings.

In taking seriously the work of literary scholars and in citing a wide range of literary examples, this book will interest not only philosophers concerned with metaphysics and the philosophy of language, but also those in literary theory interested in these foundational issues.

Amie Thomasson is Assistant Professor of Philosophy at Texas Tech University.

CAMBRIDGE STUDIES IN PHILOSOPHY

General editor   ERNEST SOSA (Brown University)

Advisory editors:

JONATHAN DANCY (University of Reading)
JOHN HALDANE (University of St. Andrews)
GILBERT HARMAN (Princeton University)
FRANK JACKSON (Australian National University)
WILLIAM G. LYCAN (University of North Carolina at Chapel Hill)
SYDNEY SHOEMAKER (Cornell University)
JUDITH J. THOMSON (Massachusetts Institute of Technology)

RECENT TITLES:

LYNNE RUDDER BAKER   *Explaining Attitudes*
ROBERT A. WILSON   *Cartesian Psychology and Physical Minds*
BARRY MAUND   *Colours*
MICHAEL DEVITT   *Coming to Our Senses*
MICHAEL ZIMMERMAN   *The Concept of Moral Obligation*
MICHAEL STOCKER with ELIZABETH HEGEMAN   *Valuing Emotions*
SYDNEY SHOEMAKER   *The First-Person Perspective and Other Essays*
NORTON NELKIN   *Consciousness and the Origins of Thought*
MARK LANCE and JOHN O'LEARY HAWTHORNE   *The Grammar of Meaning*
D. M. ARMSTRONG   *A World of States of Affairs*
PIERRE JACOB   *What Minds Can Do*
ANDRE GALLOIS   *The World Without the Mind Within*
FRED FELDMAN   *Utilitarianism, Hedonism, and Desert*
LAURENCE BONJOUR   *In Defense of Pure Reason*
DAVID LEWIS   *Papers in Philosophical Logic*
DAVID COCKBURN   *Other Times*
RAYMOND MARTIN   *Self-Concern*

Fiction and Metaphysics

AMIE L. THOMASSON

CAMBRIDGE
UNIVERSITY PRESS

CAMBRIDGE UNIVERSITY PRESS
Cambridge, New York, Melbourne, Madrid, Cape Town, Singapore, São Paulo

Cambridge University Press
The Edinburgh Building, Cambridge CB2 8RU, UK

Published in the United States of America by Cambridge University Press, New York

www.cambridge.org
Information on this title: www.cambridge.org/9780521640800

First published 1999
This digitally printed version 2008

A catalogue record for this publication is available from the British Library

Library of Congress Cataloguing in Publication data
Thomasson, Amie L. (Amie Lynn), 1968–
Fiction and metaphysics / Amie L. Thomasson.
p.   cm. – (Cambridge studies in philosophy)
Includes bibliographical references.
ISBN 0-521-64080-6
1. Fictions, Theory of.   2. Metaphysics.   I. Title.   II. Series.
BC199.F5T48   1999
111 – dc21   98–26456
CIP

ISBN 978-0-521-64080-0 hardback
ISBN 978-0-521-06521-4 paperback

for Peter

Contents

Acknowledgments

I began working on fiction during a 1993 stay at the University of Salzburg, Austria, where I had the opportunity to present some very early ideas about fiction to a lively and collegial Institute for Philosophy. As I began to see the vast implications the study of fiction has for metaphysics the work expanded, and it has been enormously improved thanks to the insight and openness of many philosophers with whom I have had the pleasure of discussing these issues.

I am particularly indebted to David Woodruff Smith; the project would have scarcely been conceivable without his insight, advice, and encouragement from start to finish. I would also like to extend special thanks to Terence Parsons and Edward Zalta who, despite the differences in our views on fiction, were always extremely generous, helpful, and fair with comments, criticism, and suggestions. Tim van Gelder, Tim Crane, Jonathan Wolff and two anonymous referees read the entire manuscript at different stages and offered numerous suggestions and comments that greatly improved the resulting work. Thanks go also to the following philosophers for helpful discussion or comments: Alan Casebier, Charles Crittenden, Greg Fitch, John Heil, Joshua Hoffman, Michael Gorman, Karel Lambert, David Pitt, Gary Rosenkrantz, Martin Schwab, Peter Simons, and Barry Smith. For moral support as well as philosophical insight I would also like to express my gratitude to Kay Mathiesen, Linda Palmer, Peter Vanderschraaf, and my colleagues at Texas Tech University.

Earlier versions of parts of this material have been previously published. A predecessor of Chapter 6 appeared as "Fiction and Intentionality" in *Philosophy and Phenomenological Research* 56 (June 1996: 277–298). Portions of my "Fiction, Modality and Dependent Abstracta" (Kluwer Academic Publishers, *Philosophical Studies* vol. 84, Nos. 2–3, December

1996: 295–320) contribute to Chapters 3 and 7 and are included with kind permission from Kluwer Academic Publishers. An earlier version of Chapter 4 appeared in *Kriterion* as "The Reference of Fictional Names" (3. Jahrgang, 1993, Nr. 6: 3–12). Finally, Chapter 5 grows out of work in two articles in *Conceptus*: "Die Identität fiktionaler Gegenstände" (vol. XXVII, 1994, Nr. 70: 77–95) and "Fictional Characters: Dependent or Abstract? A Reply to Reicher's Objections" (vol. XXIX, Nr. 74, 1996: 119–144). Thanks to the editors of *Philosophy and Phenomenological Research, Philosophical Studies, Kriterion* and *Conceptus* for permission to include this material.

Finally and most importantly, I wish to thank my husband and friend, Peter Lewis, for making the diagrams throughout the text, for serving as a constant partner for philosophical discussion and occasional editor and critic, and most especially for his unwavering love and support. The book is dedicated to him.

Introduction: From Fiction Into Metaphysics

Although examples from fiction and mythology have long provided a source of interesting puzzles and counterexamples that have guided the development of theories from Frege to Russell to Kripke, fiction has been seen as a sideshow issue in metaphysics. Even the Meinongian minority, which has done much to bring the topic of fiction back into discussion, has done little to dispel the image of fiction as a strange metaphysical jungle beyond the boundaries of traditional metaphysics.

Lying behind the sideshow view of fiction is an assumption shared by believers and disbelievers in fictional objects alike: Fictional characters are (if anything) odd, freakish entities, quite unlike common or garden objects. Disbelievers have used the supposed freakish nature of fictional entities as grounds for rejecting them, alleging that they would be too unruly to accommodate in a theory and fearing that by handling such oddities we will be led into contradiction. Believers have boldly, smilingly embraced their odd creatures, proposed special ontological realms to house them, and shown how, by handling them carefully, we can accommodate their curious tendencies and avoid contamination by contradiction.

The key to seeing the centrality of fiction in metaphysics lies in giving up this assumption and recognizing the similarities between fictional objects and other entities. In the view I propose here, fictional characters are abstract artifacts – relevantly similar to entities as ordinary as theories, laws, governments, and literary works, and tethered to the everyday world around us by dependencies on books, readers, and authors. I argue that taking fictional characters to be abstract artifacts not only provides a better way of understanding fictional characters, it also makes the study of fiction of more central relevance to other issues in metaphysics.

For, as cultural artifacts and as abstract entities, fictional characters are not alone. Like fictional characters, other artifacts from tools to schools and churches present difficulties such as how to lay out clear identity conditions for them, and how to analyze the relationships they bear to basic physical entities and to the practices and intentional acts of the individuals who create them and the communities of which they form a part. Solving such problems for fictional characters thus shows a route for solving these problems for other cultural artifacts, abstract or concrete.

Still less does their abstractness place fictional characters in a unique position. Instead it lands them in the same waters as such diverse entities as numbers, universals, laws, theories, and stories. Postulating any such abstracta leads to problems for those wishing to offer even partially naturalistic accounts of reference and knowledge. Once again, resolving these problems for fictional characters shows a path via which such difficulties may be avoided for a variety of abstract entities.

Perhaps most significantly, by combining both characteristics – by being both abstract entities and created artifacts – fictional characters fall firmly between traditional divisions of entities into the categories of concrete physical particulars and ideal abstracta. Properly accounting for fictional objects and other abstract artifacts demands breaking out of traditional category schemes that rest on bifurcations between the real and the ideal or the material and the mental. A finer-grained system of categories is required not only to accommodate fictional characters but also to do justice to the great variety of entities in the everyday world, from concrete cultural artifacts, to social institutions, to abstracta such as theories, laws, and works of music.

Treating fiction as a metaphysical sideshow is unfortunate not merely for fiction but also for metaphysics. For serious study of fiction reveals the inadequacies of traditional category systems, demonstrates how to handle other abstract artifacts, and provides occasion to reexamine the old question of what to admit into one's ontology. Based on the results from studying the case of fiction, I close by sketching an answer to the question of what we should bring into our ontology. By allowing for mental states, spatiotemporal objects, and things that depend on them in various ways, we can, from a relatively spare basis, account for a far wider range of things than is usually recognized: a true ontological bargain. One important advantage of this picture is its ability to offer a better analysis of cultural entities and abstract artifacts generally, among them the fictional objects that serve as our starting point. And so what seemed like a small corner of metaphysics – the problem of fictional objects – provides the seed to develop a new comprehensive metaphysical picture better able to do justice to the wide variety of entities in the world around us.

Part One

The Artifactual Theory of Fiction

Foreword

Discussions of fiction typically begin with the question of whether or not we must postulate fictional objects, with the defender of fiction attempting to establish that we absolutely cannot do without them, and the opponent attempting to show how we can manage to avoid postulating them through paraphrasing our apparent discourse about them and reconceiving our apparent experience of them. I believe that this approach to fiction is misguided on two counts.

It is misguided, first, to address the question of whether we should postulate fictional objects without first understanding what sorts of things they would be. We cannot see the potential costs and advantages of bringing fictional entities into our ontology until we have a clear conception of what sorts of entities fictional characters would be and how they would compare with other entities we might bring into our ontology. Vague fears that fictional characters would be too disorderly, too strange, so that postulating them would be liable to get us into trouble often drive decisions to avoid fictional objects at all costs. But we can only address whether such fears are grounded on the basis of understanding what these entities would be. Thus I propose that in Part One we postpone the question of whether or not there are such things as fictional objects, and begin by considering an easier question: If we were to postulate fictional objects, what would they be? In answer to this question I begin to draw out the *artifactual theory* of fiction. Because, in this view, fictional characters turn out to be paradigmatically dependent objects, indeed entities dependent on a variety of entities in a variety of ways, the main tool needed to develop this view of fictional characters is a theory of dependence. After making use of this theory of dependence to draw out in greater detail the view of fictional characters as abstract artifacts, I address how such a

3

view can handle two central problems ordinarily seen as stumbling blocks to postulating fictional characters: How to refer to them, and how to offer identity conditions for them. Drawing out solutions to these purported problems relieves fears that incline some to reject fictional objects and serves to fill in the details of how the artifactual theory works so that we can better examine the costs and benefits of postulating fictional characters.

It also is misguided to conceive of the game in discussions of fiction as establishing whether we can or cannot do without fictional characters. Properly considered, the question of whether we should admit anything into our ontology should not be cast as a question of whether we could possibly, through radical reinterpretations of experience and language, avoid postulating them. Making ontological decisions is a balancing act; we need to know not whether one can possibly eliminate fictional characters, but rather whether one can offer a better theory overall with them or without them. To properly evaluate the situation, we need to attempt a balanced evaluation of postulating and nonpostulating theories in terms of their ability to analyze adequately our experience and language, and to weigh this against their relative ontological parsimoniousness and elegance. In Part Two I return to address the question of whether, on balance, we should or should not postulate fictional characters as they are described in Part One.

1

If We Postulated Fictional Objects, What Would They Be?

If we are to postulate fictional characters at all, it seems advisable to postulate them as entities that can satisfy or at least make sense of our most important beliefs and practices concerning them. Often theories of fiction are driven not by an independent sense of what is needed to understand talk and practices regarding fiction, but rather by a desire to show how fictional characters may find their place in a preconceived ontology of possible, nonexistent, or abstract objects – to demonstrate one more useful application of the ontology under discussion, or to provide catchy and familiar examples. Instead of starting from a ready-made ontology and seeing how we can fit fictional characters into it, I suggest that we begin by paying careful attention to our literary practices so that we can see what sorts of things would most closely correspond to them. I thus begin by discussing what sorts of entities our practices in reading and discussing works of fiction seem to commit us to, and I draw out the *artifactual theory* of fiction as a way of characterizing the sort of entity that seems best suited to do the job of fictional characters.

WHAT FICTIONAL CHARACTERS SEEM TO BE

Fictional objects as I discuss them here include such characters as Emma Woodhouse, Sherlock Holmes, Hamlet, and Tom Sawyer – characters who appear in works of literature and whose fortunes we follow in reading those works.[1] In our everyday discussions of literature we treat fictional characters as created entities brought into existence at a certain time through the acts of an author. If someone contended that George Washington was a great fan of Sherlock Holmes, we might object that in Washington's time there was no Sherlock Holmes – the Holmes character was not created until 1887. The term "fiction" derives from the Latin *fingere* meaning "to form," and this linguistic root is still evident in our practices in treating fictional characters as entities formed by the work of an author or authors in composing a work of fiction.[2] We do not describe authors of fictional works as discovering their characters or selecting them from an ever-present set of abstract, nonexistent, or possible objects. Instead, we describe authors as inventing their characters, making them up, or creating them, so that before being written about by an author, there is no fictional object. Taking authors to be genuinely creative as they make up fictional characters is central to our ordinary understanding of fiction. One of the things we admire about certain authors is their ability to make up sympathetic, multidimensional characters rather than cardboard cut-outs, and at times we count our good luck that certain characters like Sherlock Holmes were created when, given a busier medical practice, Arthur Conan Doyle might never have created him.

Thus, if we are to postulate fictional characters that satisfy our apparent practices regarding them, it seems that we should consider them to be entities that can come into existence only through the mental and physical acts of an author – as essentially created entities. Once we begin to treat fictional characters as created entities, a further issue arises. Do they simply need to be created at some time, by someone, or is the identity of a fictional character somehow tied to its particular origin in the work of a particular author or authors taking part in a particular literary tradition? Unexamined intuitions may provide no clear answer to this question, but our goal is to draw out a view of fictional characters that corresponds as closely as possible to our practices in studying fictional characters. Such critical practices provide grounds for taking the latter view, that a particular fictional character not only has to be created but is necessarily tied to its particular origin.

Suppose that a student happens on two literary figures remarkably similar to each other; both, for example, are said to be maids, warding off attempts at seduction, and so on. Under what conditions would we say that these are works about one and the same fictional character? It seems that we would say that the two works are about the same character only if we have reason to believe that the works derived from a common origin – if, for example, one work is the sequel to the other, or if both are developments of the same original myth. Literary scholars mark this difference by distinguishing "sources" drawn on by an author in composing a work from coincidentally similar characters or works, mere "analogs." If one can show that the author of the latter work had close acquaintance with the earlier work, it seems we have good support for the claim that the works are about the same character (as for example in the Pamela Andrews of Richardson's and Fielding's tales). But if someone can prove that the authors of the two works bore no relation to each other or to a common source but were working from distinct traditions and sources, it seems that the student has at best uncovered a coincidence – that different individuals and cultures generated remarkably similar analogous characters.

So it seems that if we wish to postulate fictional objects that correspond to our ordinary practices about identifying them, fictional characters should be considered entities that depend on the particular acts of their author or authors to bring them into existence. Naturally the process of creating a particular character may be diffuse: It may be created by more than one author, over a lengthy period of time, involving many participants in a story-telling tradition, and so on. But the fact that the process of creating a fictional character may be diffuse does not disrupt the general point that, whatever the process of creation for a given character may be, for coming into existence it depends on those particular creative acts. Such a requirement not only is consistent with critical practices in identifying characters but also (as we see in Chapter 5) is crucial to treating characters as identical across different sequels, parodies, and other literary developments.

Once created, clearly a fictional character can go on existing without its author or his or her creative acts, for it is preserved in literary works that may long outlive their author. If we treat fictional characters as creations invented by authors in creating works of literature, and existing because of their appearance in such works, then it seems that for a fictional character to be preserved, some literary work about it must remain in existence. And so we have uncovered a second dependency: Characters depend on the creative acts of their authors in order to come into existence and depend on literary works in order to remain in existence.[3] Here again the question arises: Does a fictional character depend on one particular literary work for its preservation, or does a fictional character need only to appear in some literary work or other to remain in existence? It certainly seems that a character may survive as long as some work in which it appears remains. If we could not allow that the same character may appear in more than one literary work, or even slightly different editions of a work, then we would be unable to account for literary critical discourse about the development of a character across different works, and we would even be unable to admit that readers of different editions of *The Great Gatsby* are discussing one and the same Jay Gatsby. In short, we would be left postulating many characters in cases in which there seems to be but one. So it seems we should allow that one character may appear in more than one work, and if it can appear in more than one work, it must remain in existence as long as one literary work about it does. Thus even if "A Scandal in Bohemia" should exist no longer, the character Sherlock Holmes can go on existing provided that one or more of the other works in which he appears remains in existence. So, although a fictional character depends on a literary work for its continued existence, it depends only on the maintenance of some work in which it appears.[4]

The dependence of a character on a literary work forces us to address a second question: If a character depends on a work of literature, what does a work of literature depend on? When can we say that a literary work exists? Because characters depend on literary works, anything on which literary works depend is also, ultimately, something on which characters depend. As ordinarily treated in critical discourse, a literary work is not an abstract sequence of words or concepts waiting to be discovered but instead is the creation of a particular individual or group at a particular time in particular social and historical circumstances. Thus, as with characters, it seems that literary works must be created by an author or authors at a certain time in order to come into existence.

Like a character, it also seems that a work of literature depends rigidly on the acts of its particular author to exist, so that, even if two authors coincidentally composed the same words in the same order, they would not thereby have composed the same work of literature. One way to see the essentiality of a work's origin to its identity is by observing that literary works take on different properties based on the time and circumstances of their creation and creator. By virtue of originating in a different place in literary, social, and political history, at the hands of a different author, or in a different place in an author's *oeuvre*, one and the same sequence of words can provide the basis for two very different works of literature with different aesthetic and artistic properties.[5] The same sequence of words appearing in *Animal Farm* could have been written in 1905, but that literary work could not have had the property of being a satire of the Stalinist state, a central property of Orwell's tale. If the same words of *Portrait of the Artist as a Young Man* were written by James Joyce not in 1916, but instead after *Ulysses* came out in 1922, that work would lack the property of exhibiting a highly original use of language, which *Portrait of the Artist* has. Two mysteries based on the same sequence of words written in 1816 and today, both ending with "the butler did it," might have the property of having a surprise ending in the former but not the latter case.

A screenplay with the same sequence of words as Oliver Stone's *Nixon*, if written in 1913, could have the properties neither of being about (the real) Richard Nixon, nor of being a sympathetic portrayal of the main character, nor of being revisionary and speculative. Similar cases could be brought to bear to show that a wide variety of aesthetic and artistic properties central to discussions of works of literature – being a work of high modernism, a parody, horrifying, reactionary, exquisitely detailed, an updated retelling of an old story – depend on the context and circumstances of creation, so that literary works may be based on the same series of words but have different aesthetic and artistic properties. In at least some cases, these properties seem essential to the literary work, e.g., being a satire seems essential to *Animal Farm* considered as a work of literature. For that reason, it seems that a literary work is best conceived not as an abstract sequence of words but as an artifact that had to be created in those original circumstances in which it was created.

Like fictional characters, literary works, once created, can clearly survive the death of their author; indeed the great majority of literary works we have today persist despite the deaths of their authors. But does a literary work, once created, always exist, or can a work once again cease to exist even after it is created? If we take seriously the view that literary works are artifacts created at a certain time, it seems natural to allow that, like other artifacts from umbrellas to unions to universities, they can also be destroyed. It would surely seem bizarre to claim that all of the lost stories of past cultures still exist as much as ever. On the contrary, one of the things that is often lamented about the destruction of cultures, be they ancient Greek or Native American, is the loss of the stories and fictional worlds they created. We treat literary tales as entities that can cease to exist, that at times take special efforts and government projects to preserve (e.g., by recording the oral folktales of Appalachia), or that may be destroyed by a temperamental author burning unpublished manuscripts. Treating works of literature as entities that may be destroyed – at least if all copies and memories of them are destroyed – seems a natural consequence of considering them to be cultural artifacts rather than Platonistic abstracta.

Yet certainly there are many who do not share the intuition that literary works may cease to exist after being created. The idea that literary works, if they exist, must exist eternally (once created) seems to me to be a hangover of a Platonism that assimilates all abstract entities to the realm of the changeless and timeless, and in particular a consequence of viewing literary works roughly as series of words or concepts that can survive the destruction of any collection of copies of them. To the extent that it is a hangover of Platonism, this position should lose its appeal if one accepts the earlier arguments that literary works are, instead, artifacts individuated in part by the particular circumstances of their creation.

Apart from a lingering Platonism, one feature of our language might incline some to the view that literary works cannot cease to exist: We often speak not of *destroyed* or *past* works, but rather of *lost* works, as if all that were missing was our ability to find these (still existing) works of ancient, careless, or temperamental authors. This language practice, however, is easily explained without adopting the odd view that works of literature, once created, exist eternally despite even the destruction of the whole real world. The explanation is simply that, because a literary work does not require any *particular* copy to remain in existence, it is hard to be certain that there is not some copy of the work, somewhere, that has survived, and with it the work of literature. Who knows what may be lurking in the basement corridors of the Bodleian Library? A formerly lost sonnet of Shakespeare's was discovered there not so long ago. Unlike in the case of a unique painting, of which we can find the ashes, we can always hold out hope in the case of a literary work that a copy of it remains in some library, attic room, or perfect memory, so that the literary work might be "found" again. (This is reinforced by noting that, although we ordinarily speak of old or ancient works as lost, in the case of a modern manuscript burned by its author, we are more prone to count the work "destroyed" than merely lost.) But none of this speaks against the idea that, provided all copies and memories of a literary work are destroyed, never to be recovered, the literary work is gone as well – or, to put it another way, the literary work is then lost not in the sense in which sets of keys are lost, but in the sense in which an exploded battleship is lost, or a doctor can lose a patient.

If we consider characters to be creations owing their continued existence to the literary works in which they appear, then if all of the works regarding a character can fall out of existence, so can that character. Thus it is a consequence of this view that if all copies of all of the works regarding some ancient Greek heroine have been destroyed, never to be recovered or recalled, then she has fallen out of existence with those works and become a "past" fictional object in much the same way as a person can become a dead, past, concrete object. If we take seriously the idea of fictional characters as artifacts, it seems equally natural to treat them as able to be destroyed just as other artifacts are.[6] Thus fictional characters as well as the literary works in which they appear may fall out of existence with the literature of a culture.

10

One objection that might be raised to the idea that both fictional characters and literary works may fall out of existence is that it seems we can still think of them, refer to them, and so on, even after their founding texts have all been destroyed. But this is no different than in the case of other perishable objects and artifacts: We may still think of and refer to people after they have died, buildings long since destroyed, civilizations long gone by. If fictional characters and literary works cease to exist, I am not suggesting that they then enter a peculiar realm of Meinongian nonexistence or that it is as if such objects never were, but rather that they become past objects just like the other contingent objects around us. The problem of how we can think of and refer to past objects is no small one but is not unique to fiction.

Ordinarily, a literary work is maintained in existence by the presence of some copy or other of the relevant text (whether on paper, film, tape, or CD-ROM). It is in this way that the literature of past ages has been handed down to our present day. But even if printed words on a page survive, that is not enough to guarantee the ongoing existence of the work. A literary work is not a mere bunch of marks on a page but instead is an intersubjectively accessible recounting of a story by means of a public language. Just as a language dies out without the continued acceptance and understanding of a group of individuals, so do linguistically based literary works. A literary work as such can exist only as long as there are some individuals who have the language capacities and background assumptions they need to read and understand it. If all conscious agents are destroyed, then nothing is left of fictional works or the characters represented in them but some ink on paper. Similarly, if all speakers of a language die out, with the language never to be rediscovered, then the literary works peculiar to that tongue die out as well.[7] Thus preserving some printed or recorded document is not enough to preserve a literary work – some competent readers are also required. If competent readers and a printed text survive, however, that is enough to preserve a literary work.

In other cases, however, we speak of a work of literature as being preserved even if there are no printed copies of the text. In oral traditions, for example, the work is preserved in memory even if it is not being spoken or heard, and (as in *Fahrenheit 451*) it seems that a work could be preserved in memories during times of censorship, even if all printed copies of it were destroyed. So even if a literary work is typically maintained by a printed, comprehensible text, it seems that such is not necessary. A latent memory of the work (disposed to produce an oral or written copy of the work, given the appropriate circumstances) may be enough to maintain it in existence.[8] Thus we can say that, for its maintenance, a character depends generically on the existence of some literary work about it; a literary work, in turn, may be maintained either in a copy of the text and a readership capable of understanding it or in memory.[9]

In sum, it looks as if, if we are to postulate entities that would correspond to our ordinary beliefs and practices about fictional characters, these should be entities that depend on the creative acts of authors to bring them into existence and on some concrete individuals such as copies of texts and a capable audience in order to remain in existence. Thus fictional objects, in this conception, are not the inhabitants of a disjoint ontological realm but instead are closely connected to ordinary entities by their dependencies on both concrete, spatiotemporal objects and intentionality. Moreover, they are not a strange and unique type of entity: Similar dependencies are shared with objects from tables and chairs to social institutions and works of art.

Artifacts of all kinds, from tables and chairs to tools and machines, share with fictional characters the feature of requiring creation by intelligent beings. But it might be thought that the way in which fictional characters are created does make them strange, for although one cannot simply create a table, toaster, or automobile by describing such an object, fictional characters are created merely with words that posit them as being a certain way. For example, because characters are created by being written about by their authors, Jane Austen creates the fictional character Emma Woodhouse and brings her into existence (assuming she did not exist before) in writing the sentence:

Emma Woodhouse, handsome, clever, and rich, with a comfortable home and happy disposition, seemed to unite some of the best blessings of existence, and had lived nearly twenty-one years in the world with very little to distress or vex her.

But the fact that a character can be created merely through such linguistic acts should cause no peculiar difficulties for a theory of fiction. It has long been noticed that a common feature of so-called conventional or effective illocutionary acts such as appointing, resigning, adjourning, and marrying is that they bring into existence the state of affairs under discussion. Thus, for example, the celebrant of a marriage pronounces a couple husband and wife, a pronouncement that itself creates the couple's new status as husband and wife.[10] More recently, it has been noticed that it is a common feature of many cultural and institutional entities that they can be brought into existence merely by being represented as existing. Searle discusses this general feature using money as the example. A dollar bill may read:

"This note is legal tender for all debts public and private." But that representation is now, at least in part, a declaration: It creates the institutional status by representing it as existing. It does not represent some prelinguistic natural phenomenon.[11]

A contract, similarly, may be created simply by the utterance of words such as "I hereby promise to." Searle even cites as a general feature of institutional reality that institutional facts can be brought into existence by being represented as existing and can exist only if they are represented as existing (62–63).[12]

What I am suggesting is a parallel with fictional characters: Just as marriages, contracts, and promises may be created through the performance of linguistic acts that represent them as existing, a fictional character is created by being represented in a work of literature. If there is no preexistent object to whom Austen was referring in writing the words above, writing those words brings into existence the object therein described: The fictional character Emma Woodhouse.[13] Thus even the feature that fictional characters may be created not through hard labor on physical materials but through the utterance of words, rather than placing them in a peculiarly awkward situation, points again to their being at home among other cultural entities. Human consciousness is creative. It is that creativity that enables us to increase our chances of survival by formulating plans and examining scenarios not physically before us. It is also that creativity that enables the human world of governments, social institutions, works of art, and even fictional characters to be constructed on top of the independent physical world by means of our intentional representations.[14]

Nor are fictional characters alone in requiring certain forms of human understanding and practice for their ongoing preservation as well as creation. It has often been argued that works of art in general are not mere physical objects but instead depend both on some instantiation in physical form (in a performance, on canvas, in a printed copy), and – for their intentional properties such as expressiveness and meaning – on the intentional acts of humans.[15] Similarly, cultural and institutional facts regarding money, contracts, and property are plausibly characterized as depending not only on certain physical objects like pieces of paper with a certain history, but also on maintaining forms of human agreement.[16] For something to be money, it is not enough that it be a piece of paper with a certain history, it must also, both initially and continually, be accepted as what people collectively agree to count as money in a particular society.

In short, on this view fictional characters are a particular kind of cultural artifact. Like other cultural objects, fictional characters depend on human intentionality for their existence. Like other artifacts, they must be created in order to exist, and they can cease to exist, becoming past objects. It is primarily in its treatment of fictional characters as ordinary cultural artifacts rather than as the odd inhabitants of a different realm that the artifactual theory differs most markedly from other ways of characterizing fictional objects. It is also their place as cultural artifacts that makes fictional objects of broader philosophical interest, for the ontology of fiction can thus serve as a model for the ontology of other social and cultural objects in the everyday world.

It may help to locate the artifactual theory in conceptual space by briefly contrasting it with other views of what fictional objects are. Some of its advantages vis-à-vis these other theories only show up when we attempt to overcome the problems of developing identity conditions for fictional objects and handling reference to and discourse about them.[17] Nonetheless, a brief comparison should help elucidate the differences between this theory and other treatments of fiction.

MEINONGIAN THEORIES OF FICTION

The most popular and well-developed theories of fiction that have been available are those broadly construable as Meinongian theories, including those that take fictional characters to be either nonexistent or abstract entities, such as those developed by Parsons, Zalta, and Rapaport. Neither Meinong's theory nor contemporary Meinongian theories are devised specifically as theories of fiction; they concern the wider realm of non-existent objects generally.[18] Nonetheless, much of the motivation for and many of the applications of Meinongian theories of nonexistent objects concern fictional objects. Many different theories have been devised that may roughly be labeled Meinongian; despite their differences, they typically share certain fundamental characteristics captured by the following principles:

1. There is at least one object correlated with every combination of properties.[19]
2. Some of these objects (among them fictional objects) have no existence whatsoever.[20]
3. Although they do not exist, they (in some sense) have the properties with which they are correlated.[21]

14

The first principle is sometimes known as a "comprehension principle," ensuring a multitude of nonexistent objects. Meinongian theories differ with respect to which properties count in principle one. Parsons's theory, for example, limits properties to simple, nuclear properties such as "is blue" or "is tall"; Zalta's theory permits so-called extranuclear properties (such as "is possible" and "is thought about") and complex properties. Meinongians also vary with respect to how nonexistent objects "have" their properties according to the third principle; for views like Parsons's, there are two kinds of property (nuclear and extranuclear), but only one kind of predication, enabling "have" to be read straightforwardly, as (in this theory) nonexistents have their properties in the same way as real objects do. For views like Zalta's or Rapaport's, there are two modes of predication; nonexistent objects have properties in a different way than their real counterparts. Although ordinary objects exemplify their properties, nonexistent objects "encode" the properties with which they are correlated (Zalta) or have them as "constituents" (Rapaport).[22]

Meinongian theories of fiction resemble the artifactual theory in that both allow that there are fictional objects, that we can refer to them, that they play an important role in experience, and so on. Moreover, Meinongians are largely to be credited with showing that consistent theories of fiction can be developed and with undermining the paradigm according to which there are only real entities (a paradigm Parsons refers to as the "Russellian rut").

But there are also important differences between the artifactual theory and any such Meinongian theory of fiction. First, the theories differ with respect to where they apply the word "exists"; I am willing to claim that fictional characters exist; the Meinongian (by principle two) grants them no existence whatsoever. But because the Meinongian famously maintains that there are such objects, that we can think of them, refer to them, and so on, this difference is largely linguistic.[23]

A deeper difference between the theories regards how many objects they say there are. Unlike the Meinongian, I do not employ any kind of comprehension principle and so do not claim that there is an infinite, ever-present range of nonexistent (or abstract) objects. In the artifactual theory, the only fictional objects there are those that are created. This points to a further difference between this view and that of the Meinongian: In the artifactual view, fictional objects are created at a certain point in time, not merely discovered or picked out. According to the Meinongian, fictional characters are merely some of the infinite range of ever-present nonexistent or abstract objects – namely, those that are described in some story.

Accordingly, if an author writes of a character, she or he is merely picking out or referring to an object that was already available for reference. Authors can then be said to discover their characters or pick them out from the broad range of objects available, but not to bring these objects into existence. They *can* be said to make these objects *fictional*, for an abstract or nonexistent object does not become fictional until it is written about. Nonetheless, the object remains the same; it simply bears a new relation to contingent acts of authoring.[24] As Parsons writes:

I have said that, in a popular sense, an author *creates* characters, but this too is hard to analyze. It does not mean, for example, that the author brings those characters into existence, for they do not exist. Nor does he or she make them objects, for they were objects before they appeared in stories. We might say, I suppose, that the author makes them *fictional* objects, and that they were not fictional objects before the creative act.[25]

In short, the only kind of creation permitted in Meinongian accounts is the author's taking an available object and making it fictional (by writing about it in a story). This, it seems to me, is not robust enough to satisfy the ordinary view that authors are genuinely creative in the sense of creating new objects, not merely picking out old objects and thereby making them fictional. By contrast, in the artifactual theory, authors genuinely bring new characters into being that were not around before – they invent their characters rather than discovering them. In short, the Meinongian might be said to offer a top-down approach to fiction that begins by positing an infinite range of nonexistent or abstract objects and then carves out a portion of those (those described in works of literature) to serve as the fictional characters. In contrast, the artifactual theory attempts to take a bottom-up approach to fictional characters by treating them as constructed entities created by authors and depending on ordinary objects such as stories and a competent audience.

As we see in later chapters (Chapters 5, 4 and 7 respectively) there are also many differences between Meinongian theories and the artifactual theory regarding identity conditions for fictional objects and how reference to and discourse about fictional objects are handled. Some shortcomings of the Meinongian view include an inability to genuinely treat fictional characters as created entities and consequent difficulties in offering adequate identity conditions for fictional characters (especially identity conditions across texts).[26] Other problems arise for Meinongian treatments of fictional discourse, notably in handling fictional discourse about real individuals. Thus, despite the merits of Meinongian theories in offering a consistent and well-developed view of fictional characters, I argue that the artifactual theory provides a better conception of them overall. The main difference underlying the two theories and responsible for the advantages I claim for the artifactual theory lies in a fundamental difference in approach, as the Meinongian sees fictional characters as part of a separate realm of abstract or nonexistent objects, disjoint from and dissimilar to that of ordinary objects, and in the artifactual theory their similarities and connections to entities in the ordinary world are taken as fundamental.

POSSIBILIST THEORIES OF FICTION

Whether in an attempt to provide a complete account of fiction or as motivation for an ontology of possibilia, an attempt is often made to locate fictional characters among unactualized possibilia. Fictional characters have long provided some of the most appealing examples of merely possible entities and have often been used in arguments in favor of postulating unactualized possibilia. Kripke, for example, uses Sherlock Holmes as an example (which he later retracts) of an entity that "does not exist, but in other states of affairs he would have existed," and Plantinga treats the view that "Hamlet and Lear do not in fact exist; but clearly they could have" as one of the most persistent arguments in favor of unactualized possibilia.[27] And at first glance it seems plausible that, even if there is no actual person who has all of the properties ascribed to Hamlet in the play, surely there is some possible person exhibiting all of those properties, making Hamlet a member of another possible world.

This is a fundamentally different approach to fiction from that of the artifactual theory, because in the artifactual theory fictional objects are not possible people but actual characters. Although it is a tempting way to accommodate fictional characters, and fictional characters may provide fun (purported) examples of mere possibilia, major problems arise if we try to identify a fictional character with that merely possible individual exhibiting all and only those properties ascribed to the character in the story. First, as has been frequently acknowledged, there seem to be simply too many possible individuals that fit the bill, and no means to choose among them.[28] For the descriptions provided in literary works fail to completely specify what the characters described in them are like, leaving indeterminate a wide range of properties such as, typically, a character's blood type, weight, diet, and mundane daily activities. Thus we run into trouble immediately if we try to identify characters with possible people, for the features of a character left open by the story could be filled out in an infinite variety of ways by different possible people. Selecting any one as identical with a particular character seems hopelessly arbitrary. On the other hand, if the character is described as bearing incompatible properties, making it an impossible object, we have not too many possibilia to do the job, but too few.

A further problem arises in that possibilist views, like Meinongian views, give us no way of accounting for the created status of fictional characters. Even if we could find a single candidate possible detective to identify with Sherlock Holmes, this would be a possible man with the property of being born in the nineteenth century, not of being created by Arthur Conan Doyle. Finally, possibilist theories, Meinongian theories, or any theories that base the identity of a character on the properties ascribed to it eliminate the possibility that there can be more than one story about a single character. For if the character is ascribed even a single different property, it is a different character. Thus these views provide no means to admit that the same character may appear in different stories, sequels, or even slightly altered new editions or translations of an old story. Perhaps it is because of such problems that this view has been far less popular among those working seriously with fiction. Indeed Kripke and Plantinga both, after considering it, reject this view. In light of these problems it seems that possible objects are not candidates well suited to do the job of fictional characters. Because this view of fiction seems hardly able to get off the ground, I do not spend much time discussing it.[29]

FICTIONAL CHARACTERS AS OBJECTS OF REFERENCE

Other views of fiction consider fictional objects mere objects of reference that we must postulate to make sense of a certain kind of literary discourse. Such views are developed by Crittenden, who treats fictional objects as "grammatical objects," and by van Inwagen, who considers fictional objects to be the "theoretical entities" referred to in works of literary criticism. These views parallel the artifactual view in many important respects, and the differences between such theories and the artifactual theory lie less in direct conflicts than simply in the artifactual theory's filling in areas left blank by the other theories. Nonetheless, there are also important differences of approach between these theories and the artifactual theory.

Working within a broadly Wittgensteinian view of language, Crittenden postulates fictional objects as (mere) objects of reference, or grammatical objects. Although he takes fictional names as referring to certain objects, he repeatedly emphasizes that the status of these objects is merely that of objects of reference, available to be referred to by readers, critics, and other practitioners of the relevant language games of fiction, although they do not exist and are "not to be understood as having any sort of reality whatever."[30]

Although Crittenden denies that fictional characters exist, many of the features he assigns to fictional characters (based on the commitments of language practices) conform to those assigned by the artifactual theory. He too takes fictional objects to be entities created by authors through writing stories, and entities that are dependent on certain kinds of intentionality and practices involving language. But he seems to take dependence as marking a sort of honorary nonexistence and is keenest to point out that fictional objects have no *independent* existence when he is trying to emphasize that they have no "sort of reality whatever." Our later investigations into dependence should give pause to those inclined to equate an entity's existing as dependent with its not (really) existing, or having no metaphysical status.

I am sympathetic to taking our language practices regarding fiction seriously. I also agree that our literary practices in general may serve as a valuable guide in developing a theory of fiction because ideally, we want to postulate fictional characters as entities that can make sense of as large a portion of common practice as possible. But Crittenden's Wittgensteinian antimetaphysical stance leads him to rely on practice too heavily and eschew talk of the ontology of fiction by replacing ontological issues with a mere discussion of practice. As he writes:

Fictional discourse has no grounding in any further metaphysical reality; this linguistic practice itself and not some independent ontological realm is the fundamental fact in any account of the status of fictional characters (69).

Thus, instead of using practice as a guide to understanding what sorts of things fictional characters would be, Crittenden allows it to constitute what is true and false of fictional characters. Even in particular cases in which substantive issues arise regarding what is true or false of a fictional character, he simply reduces the issue to one of inquiring after our current practices. Thus he reduces the truth-values of claims about fictional characters to the accepted practices regarding their truth or falsehood, for example writing:

Such [fictional] objects . . . have properties just in that property-attributing expressions are appropriately applied to them in types of discourse such as fiction and myth. Whether these expressions are truly or falsely applied depends on purely linguistic or conceptual considerations and not on external, independent reality (97).

But in talking about fiction we should recognize that here, as else-where, we could – even as a group – be wrong. We could be wrong, for example, regarding whether characters treated as identical really are, and we could be wrong regarding the attributes we commonly ascribe to a character. Our practices themselves appeal to features beyond practice to decide issues of substance regarding the identity and properties of a fictional character – features like the character's origin. Crittenden himself occasionally acknowledges the important role played in character identity by external criteria such as the history behind the writing of the stories (43–44). Using these criteria to determine the identity conditions for fictional characters requires a willingness to reach beyond practice to discuss what the objects that would justify our practices and revisions of our practices would be like. It also requires that we treat fictional characters as more than mere objects of reference – as objects (albeit dependent ones) able to make true or false, reasonable or unreasonable, our claims and practices regarding them. The move to a detailed ontological discussion of fictional objects, not just practices regarding them, is still required.

Among current analytic treatments of fiction, that closest to the arti-factual theory is perhaps that which van Inwagen develops, according to which fictional characters are "theoretical entities of literary criticism."[31] In treating fictional characters as the entities described in literary criticism, van Inwagen rightly emphasizes the importance of postulating fictional characters to make sense of critical discourse about them. The two posi-tions coincide at many points, first and foremost in the claim that fictional characters exist.[32]

The most important difference between the artifactual theory and van Inwagen's, like that between it and Crittenden's, lies in the fact that van Inwagen does little to describe the ontological status of the creatures of fiction he postulates. He describes fictional characters as "theoretical entities"; theoretical entities in general he describes only as those referred to by the special vocabularies of theoretical disciplines, and which make some of those sentences true. So, in the case of creatures of fiction:

[S]ometimes, if what is said in a piece of literary criticism is to be true, then there must be entities of a certain type, entities that are never the subjects of non-literary discourse, and which make up the extensions of the theoretical general terms of literary criticism. It is these that I call "theoretical entities of literary criticism."[33]

This, however, does not tell us what fictional characters are like, but only that they are the things that make at least some (which?) of the sentences of literary criticism true. He does not discuss, for example, whether or not they are created, whether they can appear in more than one text, or how they relate to readers, and so we have no way of offering identity conditions for them or of evaluating the truth-value of critical sentences apparently about them. We also have little way of knowing how these creatures of fiction compare with other sorts of entities. Van Inwagen places them in the same category as other entities discussed in literary criticism such as plots, novels, rhyme schemes, and imagery, but it is not clear how they compare with other types of entities such as works of music, copies of texts, and universals. Thus we are left with no means of fitting fictional characters into a general ontological picture or of determining the relative parsimony of theories that do and do not postulate them.

I suspect that the omission of such aspects of a genuine metaphysical theory of fiction is no accident, for both theories attempt to hold a largely deflationary account of fictional characters as entities we must postulate merely to make sense of certain odd types of (theoretical or fictional) discourse; Crittenden at least would see asking such metaphysical questions as going astray in taking these mere objects of reference too ontologically seriously. Both such accounts thus still treat fiction (and for van Inwagen, theoretic discourse generally) as presenting a special case in which we must posit theoretic objects or mere objects of reference to make sense of our discourse. In this respect both theories differ importantly from the artifactual theory because, in this view, fictional characters are not to be considered theoretic entities or mere objects of reference any more than tables and chairs, committee meetings, and works of art are. Instead they are a certain type of object referred to, and indeed not a peculiar type of object but a type of object relevantly similar to stories, governments, and other everyday objects.

FICTIONAL CHARACTERS AS IMAGINARY OBJECTS

One view that has a certain similarity in spirit to the artifactual theory, although the two differ in substance, is the view that treats fictional characters as imaginary objects – entities created and sustained by imaginative acts. It is a view developed, for example, by Sartre in his work on the imagination, which he takes to apply not only to imagined objects but also to objects represented in works of art, and even to works of art themselves. An imagined object, in this view, is an entity created in an imaginative act of consciousness and that exists only as long as it is being imagined. As Sartre writes:

We have seen that the act of imagination is a magical one. It is an incantation destined to produce the object of one's thought, the thing one desires.... The faint breath of life we breathe into [imaginary objects] comes from us, from our spontaneity. If we turn away from them they are destroyed.[34]

Such a view is similar in spirit to the artifactual theory in that both insist that fictional characters are created objects, indeed objects created by the intentional acts of their authors. They are likewise similar in that both take fictional characters to remain dependent even after they are created.

But Sartre's view, and similar views of imaginary objects, treat them as existing only as long as someone is thinking of them. As a result two large problems confront this view *qua* theory of fiction. First, the idea that these objects exist only as long as they are being thought of runs counter to our usual practices in treating Holmes, Hamlet, and the rest as enduring through those periods of time in which no one is imagining them. It seems to have the odd consequence that such characters "flit in and out of existence."[35] Second, if, as Sartre has it, a fictional character is not only created by the author's imaginative acts but (re)created afresh by the imaginative acts of each reader, it is difficult to see how we can legitimately say that two or more readers are each reading about or experiencing one and the same fictional character.

It was Ingarden who first suggested how to avoid these problems and still conceive of fictional characters as, in some sense, dependent on intentionality. In Ingarden's view, a fictional character is a "purely intentional object," an object created by consciousness and having "the source of its existence and total essence" in intentionality.[36] More precisely, a fictional character is created by an author who constructs sentences about it, but it is maintained in its existence thereafter not by the imagination of individuals, but by the words and sentences themselves. Words and sentences have what Ingarden calls "borrowed intentionality," a representational ability derived from intentional acts that confer meaning on phonetic (and typographic) formations. Thus, although fictional characters remain mediately dependent on intentionality, the immediate dependence of fictional characters on words and sentences gives them a relative independence from any particular act of consciousness:

Both isolated words and entire sentences possess a borrowed intentionality, one that is conferred on them by acts of consciousness. It allows the purely intentional objects to free themselves, so to speak, from immediate contact with the acts of consciousness in the process of execution and thus to acquire a relative independence from the latter (125–126).

Because these pieces of language are public and enduring, different people may all think of one and the same fictional character, and the character may survive even if no one is thinking of it provided its representation in such pieces of language remains. In sum, Ingarden showed the way to acknowledge the consciousness-dependence of fictional characters without losing their status as lasting, publicly accessible entities; his work provides the true historical predecessor of the theory here defended.

The artifactual theory similarly avoids the problems of Sartre's view by noting that, although the intentional acts of an author are required to bring a fictional character into existence, it is not the case that it exists only for as long as someone imagines it. On the contrary, fictional characters are ordinarily maintained in existence by the existence of some copy or copies of the literary work concerning them. Although that literary work requires the ongoing existence of a community capable of reading and understanding the text, it does not require that someone constantly be reading it or thinking of it in order to remain in existence, just as the ongoing existence of money requires a community willing to accept it as money although it does not constantly require that someone be explicitly thinking "this is money." Thus literary characters on this model do not flit in and out of existence depending on whether people are thinking of them; they exist as long as literary works regarding them remain. Moreover, fictional characters on this view are not created afresh with each person's thinking of them; on the contrary, by reading the same work many different readers may all access one and the same fictional object.[37]

2

The Nature and Varieties of Existential Dependence

I have argued that fictional characters are dependent objects, requiring for their very existence such entities as literary works and the creative acts of an author. But they depend on these in different ways – requiring the creative acts of an author only to come into existence, and works of literature to remain in existence – so that it is misleading to simply speak of these indifferently as dependencies. To unravel the details of the status of fictional objects we must step back to examine the concept of existential dependence in general and to delineate carefully the various forms that this relation can take.

One should not be misled, however, into thinking that only those tracking fictional objects and other ontological oddities need to worry about dependence. Dependence is an extraordinarily common and varied phenomenon. Clear notions of dependence are important to understanding the status not only of fictional objects but also of cultural and institutional entities and certain biological, physical, and even abstract objects. Thus, showing what notions of dependence underlie this view of fictional characters reemphasizes the fact that fictional objects are to be understood along the same lines as many, perhaps most, other entities in the everyday world. At the same time, developing the tools needed to understand fictional objects provides the tools to analyze the structure of a great variety of entities of other sorts.

Before we can use dependence to explicate the ontological status of fictional characters and other objects, we need a theory of dependence at once general enough to cover all of the cases, revealing what they have in common, and fine-grained enough to respect important differences in types of dependence. Although the notion of dependence reaches back at least as far as Aristotle, contemporary work on dependence grows out

24

of Husserl's work in the *Logical Investigations*, in which he offers several definitions of foundation, a dependence relation between one entity and another without which it could not exist. Study of Husserl's work on dependence has brought about a recent resurgence of interest in dependence and awareness of the centrality of dependence to resolving various ontological issues. Work growing out of this Husserlian tradition has done much to clarify and refine different definitions of a variety of relations involving dependence.[1]

But although recent studies in dependence have made strides in clarifying the concept of dependence and bringing dependence into current discussion, they typically suffer from three problems that prevent them from serving as sufficiently general and detailed theories of dependence: First, they frequently intermix issues of dependence with other issues like part and whole, identity and difference; second, they often lack sufficient generality to include dependencies among states of affairs, characteristics of an object, and properties; and third, they fail to take into account important variations in the dependence relation, especially those variations that may be distinguished if time is taken into account.

The first step in offering a theory of dependence is to identify what the different instances of dependence have in common, so that dependence may be understood as a unified phenomenon in spite of varying cases. I shall limit myself here to discussing existential dependence, which is often defined in its basic form as: Necessarily, if α exists, then β exists. This conditional seems to place a useful necessary condition for α depending on β. Nonetheless, like mere counterfactual definitions of causality, it is insufficient to capture the full metaphysical relation. For the counterfactual may be true of α and β although they nonetheless fail to be involved in any genuine ontological relation, for example if β is a necessary existent.[2] Nonetheless, working from the counterfactual definition of dependence should provide a useful approximation of the idea of dependence that can be used to spell out important variants of the basic dependence relation and should not lead us astray if we bear in mind that it is only a formal approximation of what is at bottom a metaphysical relation.

Next, it is important to isolate the phenomenon of dependence in order to avoid the confusion that results by intermixing it with other issues. Historically, dependence has often been confused with or treated together with other formal-ontological issues. In pioneering work on dependence by Husserl and Ingarden, issues of dependence are mixed with those of part-whole relations. Although it corrects this problem, contemporary work on dependence frequently rules out cases in which the supporting and dependent entity are identical, again mixing other ontological issues with the question of dependence per se. Although it may be obvious (too obvious to be mentioned in most ordinary speech about dependence, perhaps), trivial, or uninteresting to note that everything depends on itself for its own existence, surely it is true. Apart from its triviality, one motivation for excluding cases of self-dependence seems to be in the interest of distinguishing so-called dependent from independent entities.[3] If everything depended on itself, then there would be no independent entities strictly speaking; by ruling out self-dependence this distinction may be maintained. As we see in Chapter 8, entities can be more clearly and appropriately classified in terms of what they depend on rather than in terms of whether or not they are dependent, so losing the ability to make such a distinction is not to be lamented, especially as allowing for self-dependence makes it possible to develop a smoother and more general account of existential dependence.

In order to avoid intermixing the issue of dependence with other issues and arrive at a general account of dependence, I leave open what other relations like identity, part-whole, or exemplification hold between the terms of the dependence relations defined. Although these differences are of the greatest importance in completely understanding the ontological structure of the terms and their relations to one another, the relation of dependence may be defined in the same way regardless of these variations.

A third goal of this study of dependence is to generalize the account to include dependencies among states of affairs, characteristics of an object, and properties. Work on dependence is often limited to discussing dependence relations that may obtain among objects. But dependencies may also obtain among states of affairs: Although Jones may be independent of the electorate in the sense that he could exist without it, the state of affairs of Jones' being mayor may depend on the actions of a certain portion of the local electorate. Properties, too, may stand in dependence relations to one another, at least in the sense that one property cannot be exemplified without another; for example, nothing can be colored without being extended. Particular properties or tropes of objects can also stand in dependence relations not only on the objects they qualify but also on other tropes or states of affairs, as the shape of a balloon may depend on the pressure of air inside it. Indeed dependence relations can hold among any of these types of entity in any combination; I draw on examples of all of these types in the explication that follows, which should provide insight into the great variety of cases falling under the rubric of dependence. To formulate a general theory of dependence, one must

26

allow for these variations. So doing enables one not only to account for a much greater variety of instances of dependence but also to define concepts such as "essential property," "essential part," "relative property," and so on in terms of the basic notion of dependence, making dependence applicable to other metaphysical problems.

These variations may be accounted for by permitting α and β in the basic definition to range over objects, properties, particular properties (tropes), and states of affairs. For simplicity I use the term "individual" to refer to individual objects, tropes, events, processes, and states of affairs. States of affairs are considered individuals rather than universals because they may instantiate universals but cannot themselves be instantiated by an individual.

Another important feature of a full account of dependence lies in carefully delineating the different forms that the relation of dependence can take in order to avoid equivocations and respect the differences that separate various cases. One important distinction that has often been made is between rigid dependence, or dependence on a particular individual, and generic dependence, or dependence on something or other of a particular type. For example, on some trope views a particular coloration trope like the red of this apple might be said to depend rigidly on the apple, but the apple depends merely generically on having some coloration trope or other (it could turn from green or to brown without ceasing to be this apple).

An equally important distinction that has seldom been made is based on the times at which one entity requires the other to exist.[4] As we have seen, fictional characters may require the creative acts of their authors in order to come into existence (although they can go on existing without them) but require some copy of the story to exist in order to go on existing. Such a distinction is not only important for understanding fiction; it also distinguishes, for example, the type of dependence characterizing artifacts on their producers and children on their parents; from that characterizing tropes on their objects and concrete cultural objects such as dollar bills on their physical foundations.

Finally, there are important differences based on the strength of the necessity involved in the claim that, necessarily, if α exists then β exists. Husserl distinguished formal necessity, a mere function of certain subject-neutral formal relations, such as that expressed in "necessarily, a whole cannot exist without its parts," from material necessity, a necessity based in the peculiarities of certain material kinds such as that expressed in "necessarily, anything colored is also extended."[5] Both of these sorts

27

of necessity should be discoverable a priori, based merely on knowledge of certain formal principles or an understanding of the material essences involved and relations among them. From the contemporary perspective of work in philosophy of mind and philosophy of science, we might also add the variant of nomological necessity, the necessity constrained by the laws of nature and discoverable empirically. Thus, for example, the dependency of everything on itself is formal, expressible abstractly (without any reference to the type of thing under discussion) as "necessarily, if α exists, α exists," as is a dependency such as "necessarily, if α & β exists, α exists." Dependencies such as that of an animal on its body, a work of architecture on a building, or a husband (*qua* husband) on a wife (*qua* wife) are material dependencies, based on the nature of the types of things involved, discoverable a priori provided understanding of what each sort of thing is, and not generalizable to things of other types. Dependencies such as that of fire on oxygen, of human beings on a certain air pressure, or (in most cases) postulated dependencies of thought on brain processes are (purported) cases of nomological dependencies based on laws of nature and discoverable through empirical research. Of these, formal dependence seems to be the strongest and to entail both of the others: Material laws of essence and laws of nature are subject to formal constraints, so whatever is formally necessary is also materially and nomologically necessary. Similarly, material necessity entails nomological necessity – the laws of nature cannot violate what is necessary based on the nature of the material kinds in question. In short, formal dependence entails material dependence and material dependence entails nomological dependence.

Much more could be said about these kinds of necessity and their variations, and perhaps more variations should be distinguished, but I leave that for another occasion. The dependencies of interest in the case of fictional characters seem to be predominantly material dependencies, based in the nature of fictional characters and literary works as such. For the remainder of this chapter I draw on examples of each of these types to give a sense of the variation. Thereafter, to simplify matters, I limit myself to discussing material dependence unless explicitly stated otherwise.

To understand dependence thoroughly and to make dependence a useful concept that we can apply to analyze subtleties like these without running all cases of dependence together, we need a ramified theory of dependence that takes into account the different variations in existential dependence. In addition to the variants in the strength of necessity, a wide range of different relations involving dependence may be defined by altering the basic definition along two dimensions of variation: 1) whether the dependence is on a particular individual (rigid), or only on there being something of a given kind (generic); and 2) variations in the time or times at which the supporting entity is required. I proceed to examine and define some important variations along these two dimensions and provide examples of each type of dependence along the way (although these are always meant to be mere examples to make the types of dependence intuitively clear and are not intended as claims about other philosophical or practical issues). I close the chapter by enumerating some important relations among these different kinds of dependence.

DEPENDENCE

The most completely general form of dependence is that described in the previous section: Necessarily, if α exists, β exists, in which the times at which each entity exists remain completely unspecified.[6] This is a very weak form of dependence, as all it requires is that, if α exists at some time, then β exists at some time (which may be prior to, coincident with, or even subsequent to first time). Each of the varieties of dependence that follows is more narrowly defined and entails this most general definition of dependence. We can begin by distinguishing constant dependence, a relation such that one entity requires that the other entity exist at every time at which it exists, from historical dependence or dependence for coming into existence, a relation such that one entity requires that the other entity exist at some time prior to or coincident with every time at which it exists.[7] These are not all of the different possible cases of dependence but merely describe some of the most interesting and general cases of dependence.

It is difficult to find actual cases that fall under this general definition of dependence but are not instances of constant dependence or historical dependence. Some dependent entities may be genuinely indifferent to the times at which their supporting entities exist: Universals are sometimes said to exist just in case they are instantiated *at some time*, past, present, or future.[8] The idea is that, although universals depend on being instantiated, they are not constantly or historically dependent on their instances because it is not necessary that their instances exist at some time prior to or coincident with the time at which the universal may be said to exist.

Other variations in the times required are conceivable, such as intermittent dependence, future dependence, and so on. Such cases as: A slight movement of the earth's crust is only a foreshock if a larger

29

earthquake follows, or an animal that is a new mutation is the founder of a new species only if it and its progeny reproduce and survive in the future, provide examples of one state of affairs (the movement's being a foreshock or the animal's being a species founder) depending on another at some time in the future.[9] Although plausible cases are hard to find, their mere possibility demonstrates that something may be dependent without being constantly or historically dependent. Nonetheless, as the most important and common cases of dependence seem to be constant dependence and historical dependence, I shall focus attention on these.

CONSTANT DEPENDENCE

The strongest and most central notion of dependence is that of constant dependence, in which "α is constantly dependent on β" can be broadly defined as "necessarily, whenever α exists, β exists." If the founding entity is a particular individual, the relation of constant dependence is rigid. For many purposes the most interesting version of constant dependence is between objects. Not only may the objects be identical (everything is constantly dependent on itself because necessarily, whenever α exists, α exists), an object may also be rigidly constantly dependent on one of its own parts or moments; for example, it might be that I am rigidly constantly dependent on my brain (necessarily, whenever I exist, my brain exists). If α is rigidly constantly dependent on β, and β is a proper part of α, we may call β an "essential part" of α. An entity may also be rigidly constantly dependent on something that is neither identical with nor a part of itself. Such constantly dependent individuals might include particularized properties, as these are often said to be constantly dependent on the objects they determine: Necessarily, whenever this redness (of this apple) exists, this apple exists.

But although the relation of constant dependence is often discussed only with regard to objects, the definition applies with equal ease to dependencies among any combination of individuals and properties. Either or both terms of the constant dependence relation may be a state of affairs. Examples might include such cases as the state of affairs *Mary's being a legal driver* being constantly dependent on the state of affairs of *Mary's license remaining valid*. This also allows that one state of affairs can be constantly dependent on another involving the same individual (i.e., α can be identical with β, as in *Jane's being a sprinter* depends on *Jane's being bipedal*), or that the two states of affairs involve the same property and two different individuals (for example, a *painted dancer's skirt being blue*

30

depends on certain *patches of paint being blue*). Finally, a state of affairs may depend rigidly on an object, or vice versa. For example, the state of affairs *Margaret Thatcher's being a woman* depends on Margaret Thatcher, and Margaret Thatcher may be rigidly constantly dependent on the state of affairs *Margaret Thatcher's being human*. If α is rigidly constantly dependent on a specific state of affairs involving itself, we may call the property component of that state of affairs an "essential property" of α. Thus, if Margaret Thatcher is rigidly constantly dependent on *Margaret Thatcher's being human*, then we can say that being human is an essential property of Margaret Thatcher.

We can further distinguish a special case of rigid dependence in which it is a *property* that is rigidly constantly dependent on a particular individual, in which property P's being rigidly constantly dependent on β is understood to mean: If there is anything whatsoever that is P at a particular time, then β must exist at that time. These examples are perhaps less interesting than they are abundant. One such case is the property of being Henry VIII's wife: Anyone's being a wife of Henry VIII requires the particular state of affairs *Henry VIII's being a man*.

The relation of constant dependence may also be generic, such that the entity α constantly requires that there is something that instantiates a given property, even though there may be no particular individual exemplifying that property on which α depends. For example, at any moment at which the United States of America exists, there must be something that instantiates the property of being a citizen of the United States, although there is no particular citizen whom the nation's continued existence requires. Objects, states of affairs, and properties may all stand in relations of generic constant dependence. In some cases α or a part of α may itself instantiate the property, in which case α can fulfill this need on its own; for example, a factory's being operative requires that there be something that is a power source, but a factory may also serve as its own power source.

HISTORICAL DEPENDENCE

In the case of constant dependence, the dependence in question is of one entity on another at every moment of its existence. An equally important and common variety of dependence, historical dependence, is at hand in cases in which one entity requires another in order to come into existence initially, although it may be able to exist independently of that entity once it has been created. This variety of dependence is weaker than constant dependence because it does not require that the supporting entity be present at all times that the dependent entity is.

If the historical dependence in question is on a particular individual, I call this "rigid historical dependence." For example, I am rigidly historically dependent on my parents; they were required in order to bring me into existence, but, once created, I can continue to exist without them. Similarly, a particular sample S of alcohol is rigidly historically dependent on a particular sample S_1 of simple sugar (if it were a numerically different batch of sugar, it would have produced a numerically different batch of alcohol, for the very atoms that make up the alcohol would have been different). But these sugar molecules need not (in fact cannot) go on existing once the alcohol is produced. Properties, too, may be rigidly historically dependent: Anyone's being the son of Adam requires that Adam himself exist at some time prior to or coincident with the time at which the state of affairs of *someone's being the son of Adam* exists, but one can go on being the son of Adam even after Adam himself has ceased to exist.

It might well be argued (in Kripkean vein) that any created entity must be created by a specific individual, not just some individual of a specified type, for the particular source of a created being's existence is part of its very essence. Queen Elizabeth, an historically dependent entity, is not simply dependent on there being some entities *like* her parents: She is historically dependent on those very parents. For Queen Elizabeth to exist, it is necessary not simply that she be created, or that she be created by some people with such-and-such characteristics, but rather that she be created by George VI and Elizabeth (more precisely: The very sperm and egg that united) themselves.[10] In light of these considerations, it might be thought that the concept of generic historical dependence is nonsensical, that an object, if historically dependent at all, is always rigidly historically dependent on a particular individual, not just on any entity meeting certain conditions.

But while rigid historical dependence may be both important and appropriate for describing such cases, however, there is still room for a concept of generic historical dependence; this may be understood as the kind of dependence an entity has on some of the necessary conditions for its creation that are not implicated in the identity of the created entity. Catalysts to reactions provide clear examples of the generic historical dependence of an object. As the molecules of a catalyst do not themselves combine with the initial chemicals to form the product, any sample of the right type will do to form the product. For example, alcohol is formed by beginning with a sample of simple sugar and mixing it with yeast, which merely acts as a catalyst for the reaction. The yeast forms no part of the final compound, but merely facilitates the reaction, so, as long as the same sugars were used, many different batches of yeast could have been used to produce one and the same batch of alcohol. So although a given sample of alcohol is rigidly historically dependent on the sugar from which it is formed, it is merely *generically* historically dependent on some yeast (or other appropriate catalyst). A suntan might serve as an example of the generic historical dependence of a state of affairs. The state of affairs of Jim's skin being tanned is such that its coming into existence at a particular time (Memorial Day) required the presence of some ultraviolet light, but there is no particular ultraviolet light that was required for this tan, and Jim's skin can remain tanned (for some period of time) without necessitating the continued presence of ultraviolet light.[11]

RELATIONS AMONG TYPES OF DEPENDENCE

With so many variations in the dependence relation – to do with necessity, time, whether or not the dependence is rigid, and what sorts of entities are the terms of the relation – it is easy to see how using the simple term "dependence" unexplicated could misleadingly hide a number of equivocations by masking important differences between the relations of dependence involved. By outlining the variations in the dependence relation and its terms, we can achieve a much more finely grained understanding of dependence and greatly increase the usefulness of the concept of dependence for various philosophical purposes.

To have a useful theory of dependence, however, we need more than just an enumeration of different forms the relation should take. We also need to know how these different forms of dependence relate to one another. The definitions alone point to certain obvious relations among the varieties of dependence under discussion.

1. If α is constantly dependent on β then α is historically dependent on β.

First, constant dependence entails historical dependence; if a party, for example, requires guests to remain in existence, then it must also require guests to come into existence, for it could not last a moment without them and so could not have an initial moment of existence without some guests at that (or some prior) time.

2. If α is historically dependent on β then α is dependent on β.

Similarly, historical dependence and constant dependence each (separately) entail dependence. For if anything depends on something to bring it into existence (or to maintain it in existence), it requires also that that thing exist at some time or other and so depends on it in the general sense.

3. If α is rigidly dependent on/constantly dependent on/historically dependent on a state of affairs involving property Q, then α is generically dependent on/constantly dependent on/historically dependent on Q.

That is, rigid dependence (of any type) on a particular state of affairs involving a property entails generic dependence (of that type) on something instantiating that property: If my being alive is rigidly constantly dependent on my heart beating, then we could also say that my being alive is generically constantly dependent on *something* beating. If nothing is beating, then I cannot be alive.

4. Dependence is transitive.
5. Constant dependence is transitive.
6. Historical dependence is transitive.

Finally, each type of dependence is transitive: If a fictional character depends on a work of literature about it and a work of literature depends on some copy of it, then a fictional character depends on some copy of work of literature about it; similarly, if I am historically dependent on my mother and she on her mother, then I am historically dependent on my grandmother. Because dependence is transitive, dependent entities may be layered: One entity may depend immediately on another, which is itself dependent on another, and so on.

Fictional characters provide an especially good motivation for drawing out a theory of dependence, because they exhibit many different sorts of dependence on many different sorts of entities, and because indeed the dependencies supporting them are layered, as they are dependent on literary works, which are themselves dependent on other entities. We can now utilize this system of dependence to return to make the earlier understanding of fictional objects more precise and detailed. The details of the theory of dependence also prove pivotal to understanding the place of fictional characters in a general system of categories in Part II. But it must not be forgotten that the phenomenon of dependence is completely general – many other types of entities seem to share each of these types of dependence; in fictional characters they are simply combined in an especially interesting way.

34

3

Fictional Characters as Abstract Artifacts

What we did before (handwritten)

In the intuitive view initially presented, fictional characters are higher-level dependent entities, indeed entities dependent in a variety of ways on a variety of entities. We can now outline precisely what those dependencies are and see that, as a result of those dependencies, fictional characters turn out to be abstract artifacts, a kind of entity often encountered yet little acknowledged. To make their ontological status clearer, I begin by using the prior work on dependence to make the intuitive version of the artifactual theory more precise and then turn to investigate how such dependent entities fit into a general modal metaphysics.

now ... (handwritten)

DEPENDENCIES OF FICTIONAL CHARACTERS

The immediate dependencies of a fictional character are first, on the creative acts of its author or authors, and second, on a literary work. Clearly the dependence of a fictional character on the intentional acts of its creator or creators is a rigid historical dependence. Its historical dependence on certain forms of intentionality signals it as an artifact, an object created by the purposeful activity of humans (or other intelligent beings). We are certainly no strangers to artifacts; on the contrary artifacts from computers to cutlery to couches are those entities that surround us most immediately in our everyday life. Yet little has been done to incorporate them into a philosophical ontology, perhaps in part because of fears that conditions for their identity would be too thorny, and in part because too little has been said about dependence on the thoughts and practices of human beings. Nonetheless, as artifacts fictional characters are importantly similar to other artifacts, and so working out the details

similar to (handwritten)

of their identity conditions and dependencies may provide an inroad to a better understanding of artifacts generally.

The second immediate dependence of a fictional character is a generic constant dependence on some literary work about it – constant because a character exists only as long as some literary work about it remains, and generic because a character may be maintained by the presence of any one of many different literary works. Because dependence is transitive, a fictional character, in turn, is generically dependent on whatever supporting entities such a literary work requires. Literary works, like characters themselves, however, are multiply dependent entities. A literary work, like a fictional character, is rigidly historically dependent on the acts of its creator, but that does not exhaust its dependencies: It also depends on some copy or memory of it and on an audience capable of comprehending it. Because its dependence is not on any particular copy of it, but only on some copy or memory of it, a literary work is merely generically constantly dependent on there being something with the relevant characteristics to count as a copy or memory of it[1]; similarly, because no particular reader is required, the need for a competent readership is a merely generic constant dependence. The dependencies on literary works and authors exhaust the immediate dependencies of fictional characters, and the dependencies on authors, copies or memories, and a competent readership in turn exhaust the immediate dependencies of literary works. Naturally that may not be the end of the line regarding the ultimate dependencies of fictional characters if, as seems plausible, competent audiences and copies of a literary work in their turn depend on other sorts of entities.

On this conception, although fictional characters are artifacts, they are not concrete artifacts like tables and chairs. For despite their dependencies on ordinary entities like copies of texts and authors, fictional characters lack a spatiotemporal location and thus are abstract in that sense. As we can establish empirically, fictional characters do not occupy the locations they may be ascribed in literary works. Anyone who expected to find Sherlock Holmes at 221B Baker Street or anywhere else in the spatiotemporal manifold would be making a very naive mistake, indeed a category mistake, by expecting Holmes to be a spatiotemporal entity (a real man, perhaps) rather than a fictional character.

Apart from the locations they are ascribed, the only other obvious candidate for the spatiotemporal location of a fictional character is to say that it is "in" the literary work and so is wherever that work is. But where are literary works? Only a copy of the literary work, not the work itself, is in a particular location. A literary work is only generically dependent on some copy (or memory) of it. So although it may appear in various token copies, it cannot be identified with any of them because it may survive the destruction of any copy, provided there are more. Nor can it be classified as a scattered object present where all of its copies are, because the work itself does not undergo any change in size, weight, or location if some of its copies are destroyed or moved.[2]

It would thus be wrong to locate fictional characters where copies of the literary works in which they appear are located, recited, or performed. We indeed say that fictional characters are "in" certain literary works, but describing fictional characters as "here" in the work of literature is at best metaphorical. To take it literally would be to make two mistakes. First, it would be to mistake the abstract literary work, which has no spatiotemporal location, with its concrete copies, which do. Secondly, it would be to mistake a (token of a) description of a fictional character for the character itself. Token descriptions of characters may be located in copies of the literary work, but the fact that a description of some entity has a particular location in no way suggests that the entity is located there as well. Such a mistake would never be made if an actual person was described in a literary work: If Nixon is described in *All the President's Men* we certainly do not thereby locate Nixon, the man, wherever a copy of this text is.

But copies of the text are the closest concrete entities on which fictional characters constantly depend. If fictional characters were rigidly constantly dependent on some single spatiotemporal entity, we might have reason to locate them where that foundation is. Because they are not constantly dependent on any particular spatiotemporal entity, there is no reason to associate them with the spatiotemporal location of any of their supporting entities.

If fictional characters cannot be located either where they are said to be according to the story, or where copies of the literary works are located, in the absence of more plausible candidates it seems best to treat fictional characters simply as entities that lack a spatiotemporal location. Indeed this is just what we do in practice: Sophisticated readers treat fictional characters as lacking any spatiotemporal location, and thus as abstract in that sense.[3] Thus fictional characters may, in brief, be characterized as a certain kind of abstract artifact.

Recognizing abstract artifacts requires going beyond a traditional one- or two-category ontology. Attempts are frequently made to posit only a one-category ontology of spatiotemporal particulars. The need for mathematical entities leads others to (sometimes grudgingly) acknowledge

37

the additional category of platonistically conceived abstracta: Timeless, changeless entities that lack a spatiotemporal location. But fictional characters and other dependent abstracta do not fit into either such category. For although these entities are abstract in the sense of lacking a spatiotemporal location, many of them depend on contingent entities and hence should not be characterized as necessary entities. Moreover, abstract artifacts are not timeless but instead are created at a particular time in particular circumstances, can change, and can once again cease to exist even after they have been created.

FICTIONAL CHARACTERS IN A MODAL METAPHYSICS

One way of showing how this view works and why it provides a better analysis of fictional characters than possibilist or Meinongian abstractist accounts is to show how fictional characters, so conceived, would fit into a general modal metaphysics. A traditional modal metaphysics involves actual concrete entities and possible concrete entities; if abstracta are included they are generally said to occupy all possible worlds. There are three standard replies to the question of which possible worlds a fictional character occupies: The disbeliever's view that there are no fictional objects in the actual world or any possible world; the possibilist view that, because fictional characters are possibilia, they are in some merely possible worlds (but not the actual world); and the abstractist view that, as abstract objects, fictional characters are members of all possible worlds (including the actual world).

Unraveling the dependencies of fictional characters provides a different answer to the question of which possible worlds a character belongs to: Each of our familiar (actual) fictional characters is a member of the actual world and of those other possible worlds that also contain all of its requisite supporting entities. So, for example, those worlds without Shakespeare are also worlds without Hamlet, Macbeth, and the rest; those worlds with no Holmes stories are also worlds lacking Sherlock Holmes; and those worlds completely lacking conscious beings are worlds altogether devoid of fictional characters. Note that this solution relies on other actual entities themselves, such as authors and their creative acts, appearing in other worlds. Thus if one takes the view that no actual individuals, but only their counterparts, exist in other possible worlds, there are by the same token only counterpart fictional characters. Only if we allow that some of their actual supporting entities appear in other worlds can we allow that actual fictional characters do so as well.

We can lay down more precise conditions for in which worlds a character is by examining the particular dependencies involved. Because a fictional character is rigidly dependent on its author for coming into existence, any possible world containing a given character as a member is a world containing that very author and his or her creative acts. Indeed we might add that because a character cannot exist before it is created by such acts, for any time and world containing a character, that world must contain the author's creative acts at that time or at some prior time. Because a fictional character constantly depends on the existence of a literary work about it, any world (and time) with a given character is also a world (and time) containing some literary work about it. But because a character may be maintained by two or more different literary works, it can appear in different literary works in different possible worlds, provided that its point of origin in the author's creative acts exists in that world, and that the literary works concerning the character may be traced back to it. So Holmes may be maintained by different literary works in different worlds: In some worlds only "The Five Orange Pips" may remain, in others only "A Scandal in Bohemia" may remain. In still other worlds in which Doyle wrote an additional Holmes story (not in the actual world), Sherlock may be maintained by that additional literary work even in the absence of the other literary works.

Assuming that an author's creative acts and a literary work about the character are also jointly sufficient for the fictional character, the character is present in *all and only* those worlds containing all of its requisite supporting entities. If any of these conditions is lacking, then the world does not contain the character, even if it may contain some of that character's foundations. If Doyle does not exist in some world, then Holmes is similarly absent. If there is a world in which Doyle's works were never translated and all of the speakers of English were killed off, leaving no one to understand or remember his works, then Sherlock Holmes also ceases to exist in that world, even if printed copies of Doyle's works remain. Or if, in some other world, Doyle's first work about Holmes was never published, leaving Doyle to give up writing, destroy all copies of the manuscript, and keep his stories a secret, then as soon as Doyle's memory ceases in that world, so does Holmes.

Treating these characters as members of the actual world and (merely) some possible worlds readily enables us to account for the apparent truth of such claims as those that, although there is such a character as Sherlock Holmes, if Arthur Conan Doyle's medical practice had been busier, Holmes might have never been created. Other common answers

to the question of which possible worlds a fictional character is in show no obvious means to account for basic truths like this. Disbelievers in fictional objects must consider the boredom of Doyle's practice of little advantage, for Sherlock exists just as little now as he would have if Doyle had never put pen to paper. Those who take fictional objects to be un-actualized possibilia or necessary abstracta can take scarcely more interest in these favorable conditions, for in these views, the possible or abstract entity that is Holmes was around as much before being authored as after. Although the events of Holmes's life may have been chronicled by Doyle, this bears no more relevance to Holmes's existence than literary works about Richard Nixon bear to his. Both views can, at best, consider these entities to be picked out and written about at a certain time but cannot consider them to be created by the acts of their authors. The ability of the artifactual theory to account for this basic belief and for the truth of claims that characters might have never come into existence make it an appealing alternative.

Moreover, the artifactual theory also enables us to discuss under what conditions there might have been other fictional characters than those that there actually are. If there is a world in which Doyle abandoned the Holmes stories and turned to write romances about a hapless carpenter, we may say that it is possible that there is a fictional carpenter authored by Doyle, existing in those worlds in which he is created by Doyle and maintained by one or more of the possible romances. But that fictional carpenter in that other world remains a merely possible fictional character, not a possible carpenter. Anyone who wishes to maintain an ontological distinction between actual and possible entities will find this of advantage. For whereas in possibilist or abstractist views, the two characters would share precisely the same ontological status, differing only in that Holmes alone is written about in the actual world (and hence is fictional there), in the artifactual theory one can treat Holmes and the carpenter as actual and possible entities respectively and thus respect the apparent ontological difference between those characters that are and those that only might have been.

FICTIONS AND OTHER DEPENDENT ABSTRACTA

I have suggested that we take fictional characters not to be merely possible entities, nor necessary abstract entities, but rather to be dependent entities present in all and only those worlds in which they find their necessary support. This solution to the problem of the place of fictional objects in

40

a modal metaphysics suggests the path to a different means of conceiving of the place of dependent abstracta generally in a possible-worlds ontology, a means that may be more appropriate for at least some kinds of abstracta, and that those with certain views about abstract entities might find congenial.

Often if abstracta are handled in a possible-worlds ontology they are treated as the occupants of *all* possible worlds – as ideal, necessary beings. But this seems odd for at least some kinds of abstract entities – entities like literary works and musical works. For these, like fictional characters, seem to be created entities, brought into being by their composer or author in particular historical and cultural circumstances, not discovered or picked out from an ever-present realm of ideal entities.[4] Recognizing the category of dependent abstracta enables us to offer a better account of entities such as fictional characters, literary works, and musical works and enables us to account for them without needing to postulate the Platonist's ideal independent objects.

Viewing all abstracta as necessary beings would also be unattractive to those who view certain kinds of abstracta as dependent – for example, to those who take an *in rebus* view of universals,[5] take a constructivist view of mathematical entities,[6] or view certain ideas as the products of cultures or individual mental acts.[7] For in such cases it would seem wrong to say that these entities are present in all possible worlds regardless of whether they are instantiated, or whether or not they have been created.

Where fictional characters are concerned, I have argued that although they are abstract in the sense of lacking a particular spatiotemporal location, they are not members of all possible worlds but only belong to those worlds containing the entities on which they depend. This solution to the problem of which possible worlds a fictional character resides in comes as a direct consequence of their status as dependent entities. The same principle applies to other dependent entities of all types: They may be found in those possible worlds in which their supporting entities reside. Thus on an *in rebus* view of universals, the universal *being red* exists in precisely those worlds in which there is something red (for it depends on being instantiated). A musical work like a symphony might exist only in those worlds containing its creator and some performance of that work. A mathematical entity, on a constructivist view, might exist in only those worlds containing mental acts of the relevant type. Similarly, a culturally local idea might exist only where it has been developed through the relevant intentional acts of a community, and a law of state might exist only where it is enacted by a legitimate legislative power.

By following this method, one can allow possible worlds to vary in what abstract entities they contain as well as in what ordinary, spatiotemporal entities they have; there can be contingent, dependent abstracta indexed according to the possible worlds in which their supporting entities reside. There are as many choices about precisely which worlds an abstract entity resides in as there are ways in which it can be, or fail to be, dependent.

Yet the suggestion that we postulate fictional objects under this conception, or any related dependent abstracta, is likely to be met with fear and resistance by many adhering to a one- or two-category ontology. There are two pressing worries that must be addressed before seriously considering admitting such entities into our ontology. One problem for those who postulate abstract entities of any kind is how we could refer to or acquire knowledge of these entities if they are not part of the causal order of spatiotemporal objects. A second problem to be addressed in considering fictional characters, or whenever we consider admitting entities of a different kind into our ontology, is whether we can offer straightforward identity conditions for them.

I turn now to showing how we may resolve these problems by treating fictional characters as relatively familiar entities connected by dependence relations to the everyday world around us. Finding clear solutions for fictional objects considered as dependent abstracta should not only help allay fears that fictional objects are too problematic to deal with but also pave the way for accepting dependence-based accounts of the ontological status of other cultural artifacts and dependent abstracta.

42

4

Reference to Fictional Characters

Dominant theories of the reference of names have emphasized that names, unlike descriptions, function by means of a direct reference to their objects, and that causal and historical circumstances play an essential role in our ability to refer to objects by name. This model seems to break down in the case of fictional names: If fictional objects are not spatiotemporally located, then it seems they must also be causally inert, making it inconceivable how causal or historical circumstance could play any role in the reference of fictional names.

This supposed incompatibility between the claim that fictional names refer and the claim that causal or historical features are essential to the reference of names has provoked many to reject the thesis that fictional names refer. Traditional causal theories of reference treat names of fictional characters as nonreferring terms, and in *Naming and Necessity* Kripke goes still further to argue that genuinely fictional names *cannot* refer to any actual or possible object.[1] Indeed, anyone who wants an even partially naturalistic account of the reference of names, taking causal or historical chains to play an essential role in the reference of names, has cause to worry about the case of fictional names. Those who take fictional discourse seriously have on occasion taken the other horn of the dilemma, maintaining that because causal or historical theories *cannot* allow that fictional names refer we should abandon an across-the-board causal-historical model of reference.[2]

Troubles with reference present difficulties for those postulating fictional objects, for if we cannot successfully refer to fictional characters at all, then there seems little point in postulating them, and the process of acquiring knowledge about them becomes mysterious. If we can refer to fictional characters, but only or primarily by means of description, not by name, then fictional names present an odd case, making fictional objects more suspect and requiring us to abandon hope for a single theory of reference applicable to both fictional and real names.[3]

This problem is not unique to fictional objects but arises for other abstract entities as well, and indeed for any purported entities lying outside of the spatiotemporal, causal order, including mathematical entities and other abstracta.[4] Thus, resolving this problem for fictional objects may point towards a possible resolution for certain other abstract entities as well.

If fictional characters are seen as the occupants of another ontological realm totally disconnected from the spatiotemporal world, then it might seem mysterious how one could allow any role for causal and historical context in determining the reference of their names. But if fictional characters are conceived as historical entities closely connected to the spatiotemporal entities on which they depend, entities as ordinary as copies of texts, then a role can be provided for causal or historical circumstance in the reference of fictional names. Although the name cannot be directly causally related to its referent if the referent is a fictional character, it can be causally related to a *foundation* of the referent (namely the text), to which in turn the referent is connected by the relation of ontological dependence, enabling one to refer to these abstracta via their spatiotemporal foundations. Indeed the basic model that Kripke offers in *Naming and Necessity* and Gareth Evans modifies in *The Varieties of Reference* of the determination of the reference of names through a "baptism" and the continuation and proliferation of the use of a name via chains of communication can be applied in a modified version to names of fictional entities – provided we allow that not only causal relations but also relations of ontological dependence can form a path for direct reference. As I argue at the close of this chapter, this is something we have good reason to do independently of concerns with fiction.

KRIPKE AND FICTIONAL NAMES

Kripke's original argument that genuinely fictional names cannot refer is implicit in some terse remarks in the addenda to *Naming and Necessity*, in which he attempts to make good on his "surprising" claim that predicates such as "unicorn" and names such as "Holmes" do not merely lack reference contingently.[5] He divides his discussion into a metaphysical thesis and an epistemological thesis. His metaphysical view is that not only is there no actual Sherlock Holmes, there is also no possible person, such that if he were actual he would be Sherlock Holmes:

> I hold the metaphysical view that, granted that there is no Sherlock Holmes, one cannot say of any possible person that he *would have been* Sherlock Holmes, had he existed. Several distinct possible people, and even actual ones such as Darwin or Jack the Ripper, might have performed the exploits of Holmes, but there is none of whom we can say that he would have *been* Holmes had he performed these exploits. For if so, which one? (158)

The basic insight behind this argument seems to be that characters presented in and invented by literary works or myths are described just by words, so all we have to determine reference is something like a description. But Kripke has argued that description is insufficient to determine the reference of names, natural-kind terms, and the like. Because of the logical form of a name, it must refer to a single individual if it refers at all. But the descriptions provided in literary works fail to uniquely determine a single real or possible individual. Indeed an infinite number of possible individuals could all match the incomplete descriptions offered in literary works and still differ from each other regarding those properties that remain unspecified in the literary work. These considerations provide good arguments against identifying fictional characters with unactualized possibilia, although, I will argue, not against fictional names having a reference.

Kripke's epistemological thesis suggests a different means of establishing that names of fictional entities cannot possibly refer. His epistemological thesis is that the mere discovery of a detective with all of the properties attributed to Holmes would not be sufficient to prove that Sherlock Holmes exists, for it could be mere coincidence. To prove that this existing individual is Sherlock Holmes we would also need a historical connection to show that Conan Doyle was referring to *this man* (which would mean having learned to use the name in an appropriate chain of communication) when he used the name in the texts.

The point behind this argument seems to be that, because names refer in virtue of the connection between the use of the name and a historical name-use practice leading back to a baptismal act, if Arthur Conan Doyle is not participating in some such practice when he uses the name "Holmes," then even if some real person answers Holmes's description, we could not say that Doyle was referring to that person in writing about Holmes and so could not identify that person with Holmes.

This means that we have a strict necessary condition for a "fictional" name's referring: "Sherlock Holmes" refers only if there is some one and only one (real) person about whom Doyle was writing when he wrote the character. This presupposes that the name can only refer if in fact the individual referred to is not fictional; it can only refer in the same way as normal names refer, by being applied in a chain of communication to a single person in the actual world (in virtue of which it then can pick out this same individual across all possible worlds). We need a baptism procedure to fix the referent of a rigid designator, but no merely possible entity can be at hand to be baptized by the author or by someone else who starts the name usage chain in which the author participates. So (because these names cannot be applied to possible things in a baptism) these names – if they are genuinely fictional names, not names applied to real people – cannot refer to anyone, actual or possible.

Kripke's later lectures on fiction, the 1973 John Locke Lectures "Reference and Existence," make it evident that the results from *Naming and Necessity* are more limited than most have taken them to be: They establish that fictional names cannot refer to any actual or possible *person*, but not that they cannot refer to actual *fictional characters*. As Kripke points out in the third lecture, there are two senses in which Sherlock Holmes could be said to exist. First, it is true that according to the story he exists; second, it is true that there is such a fictional character. Although originally in the telling of fictions there is merely a pretense that names such as "Sherlock Holmes" refer, ordinary language eventually supplies a referent by inventing an ontology of fictional characters. Such characters, Kripke argues, should be understood as contingent and "in some sense" abstract entities in the actual world existing by virtue of activities of storytelling and identifiable on the basis of their historical origins in storytelling practices. As far as one can tell from the brief remarks of a single lecture, this seems to be a view of fictional characters in many ways similar to that defended here. But, as Kripke never expanded on these suggestions or chose to publish these lectures, his settled view on these matters may only be conjectured. In any case, having allowed that names such as "Sherlock Holmes" may refer to abstract fictional characters, he does not go on to show how this reference may be established and maintained on a causal-historical model such as his own. That remains to be done here.

BAPTISM OF FICTIONAL OBJECTS

Kripke's original arguments in *Naming and Necessity* are partly right: Provided Arthur Conan Doyle was not participating in an established naming practice to refer to a real person, there is no *real* (spatiotemporal) thing to which the term "Holmes" refers, even if someone happens to match those descriptions. Moreover, there is no possible man to whom it refers. But this does not show that "Holmes" cannot possibly refer.

Although the earlier Kripke work is right in claiming that genuinely fictional names do not refer to any actual or possible people, as he later acknowledged himself, it would be wrong to conclude that fictional names cannot refer. To arrive at that conclusion one would have to unjustifiedly assume (1) that fictional works merely provide us with descriptions; (2) that, because there is no spatiotemporal thing to be baptized there can be no baptism process, and hence no rigid reference (of the sort names require); and (3) that if fictional names refer, they must refer to some actual or possible person. If we give up the idea that fictional names refer to actual or possible people and turn to the idea that they instead refer to a kind of abstract artifact, the issue becomes very different.

The whole idea of baptizing fictional objects and other nonspatiotemporal entities has often been presented as absurd – for surely in these cases there is nothing to point at and name.[6] I can point at the child I name "Richard Nixon" and thus fix the reference of that name in all possible worlds; but there is nothing that either I or Virginia Woolf or anyone else can point at to declare, "This is called Clarissa Dalloway," nor is there (normally) anything answering to an initial description that we could give to pick out an object in the first place and assign it a name. This, however, shows not that there is no baptism process for fictional characters, but only that it must be conceived of differently than that for spatiotemporal objects.[7]

Although there can be no direct pointing at a fictional character on the other side of the room, the textual foundation of the character serves as the means whereby a quasi-indexical reference to the character can be made by means of which that very fictional object can be baptized by author or readers. Something counting as a baptismal ceremony can be performed by means of writing the words of the text or it can be merely recorded in the text, or (if the character is named later, for example by readers), it can remain unrecorded in the text.[8]

Perhaps the most typical case of naming a fictional character (although it is by no means necessary that naming should occur in this way) is the case wherein an author names her or his character in the text in which he or she appears. The textual use of the name of a fictional character in the context of a description in a work of fiction serves as a kind of indexical reference to the character founded on those very words of that very narrative. Often the use of a name in conjunction with words describing the character being written itself constitutes an "official" baptism of the character. For example, in the opening pages of George Eliot's *Silas Marner* we read: "In the early years of this century, such a linen-weaver named Silas Marner worked at his vocation in a stone cottage that stood among the nutty hedgerows near the village of Raveloe, and not far from the edge of a deserted stone pit." When the name "Silas Marner" is here employed it is as if it were to say, for example, "the character founded on these very words is to be called 'Silas Marner'," so that the very use of the name in the text constitutes a naming ceremony, or at least an official and public record thereof. The intratextual naming ceremony can take place at any point in the writing or revision process, from the initial stages of beginning to develop and introduce a character, through to the stages of final revision in which a name is changed or given to a previously unnamed character. It is with good reason that the naming ceremony is normally recorded in the text, for this allows the character to be reidentified at various points and across various descriptions in the text; the recording of the baptism in the text corresponds to the requirement that the naming ceremony be somehow public.

The stage of the writing process during which the character is named can, of course, vary greatly: An author can choose a name before even beginning to write a character, name a character while it is being developed, or add a name to a previously unnamed character late in the process of revision. But the problems here are no different in kind from those of naming real individuals, for whom there may be no single identifiable ceremony, and the name can be applied at any stage in a person's life. The notion of a "baptismal ceremony" here, as in Kripke's original account, must be taken somewhat loosely and metaphorically, as part of a general picture under which a name is applied to an individual somehow publicly and in which the name is then passed along in communicative chains that refer back rigidly to this individual.

Although the paradigm case of naming involves recording that name in the text, there is no reason in principle why a character's naming should have to be performed by its author or recorded in the text, and whether from oversight or for suspense, style, or innovation, there are countless examples in literature in which a fictional object is left unnamed in the text, to be named later if at all. In some cases, there is an identifying description of some kind that serves as a kind of name to keep track of the character until the naming practice associated with some identified character is grafted onto it. The identifying description, if it is unique given the context and used consistently to identify a single character ("the gray-eyed woman"), can itself function nonproblematically as the name of that character, as there is of course no reason in principle that a fictional character (or anyone) be named with something resembling a standard proper name.

More difficult cases also arise, however, in which there seems to be a single character who is identified not by a single name or unique and repeated description but is only unifiable by certain patterns of behavior, of dress, of speech, or of the descriptions associated with it. This, for example, is the case in the first half of Stephen Fry's *The Liar*, in which the characters in the italicized portions of the text are given neither names nor fixed descriptions but are merely described in terms of the clothes they are wearing on that occasion. The clothes change, so there is no fixed description to act as a pseudo-name; the reader can unify these characters only by recognizing certain patterns in style of dress.[9] In such cases the naming process may come later, by a sort of consensus among readers and critics rather than by the stipulation of the author. This has occurred, for example, with the "dark woman" of Shakespeare's sonnets. This of course requires a sort of public identification process of the character to be baptized, but as long as the readers can, through discussion, agree on the character they mean, at least in part by identifying the literary work in which it appears (whether by description or ostension) and the passages of the text that describe the character to be named, this should not be a problem. The chain of reference of the name then begins later but still refers to that very character created by that very author in the literary work in question, just as a real person could be given a name relatively late in life. Once again, it is by way of the textual foundation of the character that one may make an indexical kind of reference to "the character founded on these words of this text" and thus perform a baptismal ceremony.

MAINTAINING A CHAIN OF REFERENCE

Once conferred on a fictional entity, a fictional name is then used in a chain of communication, much like proper names of ordinary people, except that the people who use a fictional name need not learn to use it just from each other but may also learn it directly from the work of literature. Kripke discusses only communicative chains wherein the name is passed "from link to link" in a given speech community, but in literature the name of a character may be passed along in a chain of publication of copies of the novel or novels in which the character appears. Like the chain of communication, the chain of publication leads back to the origin of the character, and normally (that is, apart from cases in which the name is conferred on the character later by readers) to the baptismal act.[10] The name of a fictional object is most frequently and most securely passed along by the printed rather than spoken word. Readers become initiated into the naming practice through reading the relevant novel; in the standard case they are "told" the name as they are introduced to the character by reading about it in the act of reading the novel.

People who have never read the work in question may also use the name to refer to the fictional character, even if they know little about that character or make (some) mistakes in the properties that they think it has, as long as their use of the name has been learned in the community that passes the use of the name along in the chain of communication and publication. This is important in explaining how it is that an outsider who has never read or seen the play *Hamlet* and could not provide a complete or accurate description of Hamlet can nonetheless use the name to refer to the same character as that referred to by a literary critic. In the case of fictional names, as in that of real names, we can follow Evans in distinguishing producers from consumers in the naming practice. Whereas, in the case of real names, the producers are those acquainted with the individual named, who can identify her or him and provide information about her or him to be passed through the communicative chain, the consumers are the parasites on the naming chain, who have some idea of the name and information associated with it, but who do not know the referent of the name. In the case of fictional names we can count as producers the competent readers of the text containing a character, who become acquainted with the character by reading about her or him. But in this case as well, there may be consumers in the naming practice who simply learn enough from the producers (and other consumers) around them to use the name properly. The most famous literary characters of any culture or era become publicly discussed by individuals who have never read the work in question; this kind of discussion is possible because the producers can pass relevant pieces of information associated with the fictional name on to nonreaders, who can learn the appropriate use of this name from readers and hence become consumers in the naming practice.[11]

Ebeneezer Scrooge of Dickens's *A Christmas Carol* is a fine example of such a character in our culture: Most contemporary Anglo-Americans know sufficient information to be competent users of this name, and even to pass along information about Scrooge to others (to teach their children that Scrooge was visited by three ghosts), even though but a small proportion of them have actually read the text.

As in the case of the names of real individuals, reference shifts in the names of fictional characters can occur even if the chains of communication and publication remain intact. Reference shifts occur if people intend to refer to a different object (perhaps thinking that it is the same object) and thereby redirect the naming practice to refer to a different entity than that initially baptized with the name. Such a shift has occurred, for example, with the name "Frankenstein," which was conferred on Mary Shelley's fictional cowardly Swiss scientist but by now has migrated in the common speech practices of American children, at least, to refer to a remorseless and stupid green monster with a bolt through its neck (rather than even to the yellow, quick-minded, and angst-ridden unnamed monster of Dr. Frankenstein's creation). Keeping the name usage chain closely tied to the chain of publication is probably the best method of ensuring against reference shifts: Shifts from a fictional to an imaginary character are most likely to occur if the name usage practice is distanced from the practices of actual producers who have read the relevant book and instead left in the hands of consumers, who are far more likely to spread false information along the naming chain.

It is hard to specify the point at which a name-use practice shifts from merely spreading false information about a certain individual, real or fictional, to the point at which we would say that it is no longer about that individual but about some mythical or imaginary entity. I should reemphasize here, however, that the problem is no different in kind for fictional than for real individuals. Moreover, in the case of fictional individuals we do have the advantage, where the longevity and accuracy of a naming practice is concerned, for we have definitive texts that can maintain an accurate naming practice (passed along primarily through copying texts rather than talking) maintained by producers for an indefinite period of time; whereas real individuals eventually die, as do the original producers of their naming practices, leaving behind only possibly unreliable documents and the hearsay of generations of consumers to carry on the practice of names of real individuals.

Whether in the case of names of real or of fictional individuals, the prevalence of reference shifts shows that the maintenance of an historical chain of name use leading back to a baptism is only a necessary, and not a sufficient, condition for a particular use of a name to refer back to the appropriate individual. Reference shifts serve as a reminder that a complete theory of reference needs to incorporate factors other than historical circumstances, including the mental contents of speakers. By admitting other factors in the reference of names, we may temper strict

causal-historical accounts without abandoning the general picture according to which historical chains and baptisms play a central role in determining the reference of a name, regardless of whether it is the name of a
real person or of a fictional character.

RESULTS FOR FICTION AND BEYOND

Providing a way to preserve a uniform account of the reference of names
demonstrates a way to preserve the central insight of direct-reference
theories: That causal and historical chains play an essential role in determining the reference of names. That essential role of causal and historical
chains is here preserved between the utterance and the spatiotemporal
foundation of the fictional character. But it also suggests that an improved
theory of reference may be devised by admitting that causal relations are
not the only things involved in achieving direct reference. By allowing
chains of reference to travel along chains of dependencies as well as causal
and historical chains we can develop a broader theory of reference that

enables us to account for reference to entities other than simple space-
time particulars in the causal order: not just fictional characters, but also
entities such as universals, stories, theories, and laws.

Have we any independent reason, however, to allow that chains of reference may travel not only along causal chains but also chains of dependencies? I believe we have two: First, that actually seems to be the way
our language practices work; second, it enables the general point about
reference to be separated from the need for a spare ontology. Our ordinary speech practices quite often appear to make use of an ability to
refer to abstract entities via the spatiotemporal concreta in which they are
exemplified or represented or on which they depend. Indeed, without
careful attention to context and speaker's intentions, we often cannot be
certain whether the entity referred to is a concrete object, one of its dependent properties, a type that it exemplifies, or even a further entity that
it represents. Pointing at a passing Studebaker, Pat remarks, "Now there's
a great car." He may be referring to the particular car, well maintained,
with a remodeled engine and extra torque. More likely, if he lacks knowledge of the particular passing vehicle, Pat is referring to Studebakers, the
model of car generally, by pointing at one on the street. In that case
his remark may be true even if the particular car in question is so badly
maintained as to belong in the junk yard.[12] One could similarly refer to
Studebakers, the model of car, by pointing not at any vehicle, but at a copy
of the factory blueprint, although here, too, there may be an ambiguity of

reference between the blueprint itself and the object represented. If Jane comments, "That's a work of genius," she may be referring to the car's remarkable design, or to the exceptionally clear way in which its specifications are recorded in the blueprint itself. Similarly, one may refer to (fictional or real) objects represented in paintings by pointing at the painting, as with a remark, "That's Jupiter," made while pointing at a cloud-like figure in Correggio's *Jupiter and Io*. In any case, quasi-indexical references to abstract entities (such as types of car) and represented objects (types of car, painted figures) via instances of them or plans and representations of them form an essential part of our use of language to discuss more than simply the particular physical objects before us. The ability to refer directly to a fictional character by means of a copy of the text in which it is represented is no different in principle than our ability to refer to a type of car represented in a blueprint, or a figure represented in a painting.

Secondly, allowing for reference to dependent entities via the spatio-temporal objects on which they depend provides a means to prevent the general point about the importance of causal and historical circumstance in reference from needing to be tied to a particular ontology. Those who adopt partially causal-historical theories of reference may be, but need not be, wedded to a spare ontology that acknowledges only particular physical entities. Those who are convinced that causal and historical chains play an essential role in the reference of names, but who nonetheless want to admit into their ontologies such entities as works of music, kinds of car, scientific theories, or legal statutes face the same problem of how to accommodate reference to these abstract entities within a theory of direct reference. Broadening traditional direct reference theories to allow chains of reference to travel along chains of dependencies as well as causal and historical chains supplies a means of understanding direct reference to dependent abstracta in general.[13] If these things are connected to the spatiotemporal world by relations of dependence, we can refer back to them via the space-time objects on which they depend. Just as one can refer directly to a fictional character via a copy of the literary work, so can one refer to Bach's Third Violin Concerto by designating a performance of it ostensively as it is aired on the radio or written in a copy of the score ("This is my favorite of Bach's works"). Similarly, one can learn about Bach's works or the Studebaker engine via direct cognitive access to these same spatiotemporal foundations (listening to performances, reading the score; repairing particular Studebakers or studying copies of plans for their engines). In each case, the context and style of phrasing make it clear that it is not the particular performance or automobile referred to but the abstract entity founded on it. Thus broadening out theories of direct reference provides a means to make the theory work for a far wider range of entities by allowing that we can achieve direct reference to and gain cognitive access to dependent abstracta by means of the space-time objects on which they depend. Anyone impressed by the role of circumstances in determining reference but not committed to barring all but particular spatiotemporal entities from his or her ontology has independent reason – apart from considerations of fiction – to broaden the theory in this way.

Once the theory is so broadened, we can develop an account of how fictional names refer to characters that disarms objections that we could not refer to or gain knowledge of fictional objects and enables us to preserve an important aspect of our discourse about fictional characters. The reputed problem of referring directly to fictional characters turns out not only to be soluble but also to show the way to resolving problems of direct reference for a host of other entities.

5

Identity Conditions for Fictional Characters

One fear that inclines many to reject fictional objects is that we are liable to get ourselves into trouble either by falling into contradiction or by trying to constrain such unruly entities into the confines of a well-behaved theory. The motivation for rejecting fictional objects on the basis of their supposed intractability goes back at least as far as Russell's claim that Meinong's nonexistent objects are "apt to infringe the law of contradiction" and has gained contemporary popularity from Quine's characterization of unactualized possible objects (and presumably other so-called nonexistents) as "a breeding ground for disorderly elements," making them unsuitable for proper individuation and untractable in philosophical theories.[1]

Those who do attempt to offer identity conditions for fictional objects generally do so by reducing fictional objects to ideal abstracta, so that their identity conditions are reduced to those of more familiar and tractable entities. But such attempts inevitably miss important aspects of our ordinary practices in counting characters as the same or different. This difficulty is not unique to fiction: Indeed, some of the stickiest problems of identity arise for other cultural artifacts such as statues and monuments, musical works, and literary works, which are not identifiable with either basic physical concreta or with ideal abstracta and which thus seem to demand identity conditions different from those for either.

By conceiving of fictional objects as abstract artifacts we can offer identity criteria for fictional objects both within and across literary works that not only are as clear and precise as those we have for ordinary objects but also correspond closely to our practices in treating fictional characters as the same or different. Moreover, the means employed to develop these identity conditions show the way for devising identity conditions for many

55

other kinds of dependent objects, including the literary works on which fictional objects depend.

TROUBLES WITH MEINONGIAN IDENTITY CONDITIONS

The most popular theories of fictional objects, Meinongian theories, have done much to answer the challenge of offering clear identity conditions for fictional characters by offering identity conditions for fictional characters that parallel those for sets and other independent abstracta. According to Parsons's Meinongian theory, for example, there is a unique object correlated with every set of (nuclear) properties, so that fictional objects x and y are identical if and only if x and y have exactly the same nuclear properties.[2] Zalta's theory of fictional objects as abstract entities offers similar identity conditions, stipulating that two abstract objects (including fictional objects) are identical just in case they encode exactly the same properties.[3] One could hardly ask for greater clarity and orderliness. Despite the admirable simplicity of the identity conditions offered, however, Meinongian theories tend to run into an array of problems in individuating fictional objects in ways that correspond to our practices in treating fictional characters as the same or different.

To make the shortcomings evident, consider the case of Pamela. Our critical practices presuppose that Richardson's Pamela of *Pamela* and Fielding's Pamela of *Joseph Andrews* concern the same character, invented by Richardson and referred to by Fielding, who attributes new properties to her in his parody. By contrast, as I argue in Chapter 1, if a student should turn up an unknown tale about a maid called "Pamela" and the attempts of a squire to seduce her, and if that tale were in no way connected to Fielding's or Richardson's work, making it pure coincidence that there were such similar characters, we would with justice regard these Pamelas as merely remarkably similar – but distinct – characters. To make the point still clearer, imagine that there is such a twin Pamela, written about one rainy afternoon in 1957 by Fred Jones, who purely coincidentally – without any direct or secondary acquaintance with Richardson's or Fielding's work – ascribed to his Pamela just the same properties that Richardson ascribed to his. Because critical practices involve identifying characters only if they stem from a common origin, however, in absence of this the two Pamelas can at most be remarkably similar. Thus one challenge for those who would offer identity conditions for fictional characters is to provide a means to tell us that Richardson's Pamela is the same as Fielding's but different from Jones's.

56

The identity conditions offered by the Meinongian can do neither. Because the circumstances of creation can play no role in the identity conditions of fictional characters, such theories must classify characters with the same properties ascribed to them as identical even if they are so created merely accidentally. Thus such theories must maintain that Richardson's Pamela and Jones's Pamela are one and the same character, ignoring the importance of historical origin in our ordinary practices of identifying fictional characters.

The case of characters ascribed exactly similar properties is so unlikely that it is not likely to raise a great deal of worry. But if a theory is unable to account for the identity of characters that appear in different works of literature, or even in slightly altered versions of the same work of literature, this presents far more serious problems. Handling transtextual character identity presents huge problems for theories that identify characters solely on the basis of properties they are ascribed. For if merely a single property is changed (for example in a new edition of the novel, in which a single word is deleted), then according to these conditions we are dealing with two distinct characters. So according to such theories distinct characters often appear where we would normally think there is but one – in texts reprinted with typographical errors, in translations, and in sequels – giving us a great horde of Jay Gatsbys, many Anna Kareninas, a long series of distinct characters all called "Sherlock Holmes," and *separate* Pamelas belonging to Richardson's tale and Fielding's parody. These consequences violate our critical practices regarding character identity and hence are unappealing solutions to the challenge of offering identity conditions for fictional objects.

Various attempts have been made to overcome this problem and enable the identification of characters across literary works without giving up the idea that characters are pure abstract entities individuated solely by their properties. The first strategy involves going to the smaller character – that shared by each of the works – so that we can say that the sense in which each work is about the same character is that, as it were, they contain a part in common (a basic figure included in all the works and expanded by each).[4] The second attempt is the opposite move: Going to the larger character (with the properties ascribed in all of the works put together), so that the sense in which the diverse works are about the same character is that they describe parts of the same whole.[5] I argue that both fail: That the first fails to offer reasonable identity conditions and leads to absurd consequences, and the second is either useless or question-begging.

The first attempt to account for the fact that one character may appear in several different literary works is developed by Wolterstorff, who offers a different abstractist view of fictional characters that nonetheless follows the same general principle of drawing out identity conditions for fictional characters based solely on the properties with which they are correlated. In Wolterstorff's view, fictional characters are certain kinds, namely person-kinds picked out by authors in writing the literary work. Thus when Gogol wrote about a character called "Chichikov," he was delineating a certain kind of person, that kind that someone belongs to just in case he exhibits all of those properties attributed to Chichikov. The properties attributed to Chichikov (as well as some others that may not be explicitly stated in the work but merely presupposed) are said to be "essential within the kind" Chichikov, meaning that if anyone is to be of the Chichikov kind, he must exhibit all of these properties.

Wolterstorff admits that this view faces difficulties in handling both the apparent identity of characters across different texts and such claims as that the author could have written the character slightly differently. For, according to Wolterstorff, there is a one-to-one function mapping properties onto kinds.[6] Thus, if different properties are ascribed to a character in a different work or if different properties were to be ascribed to a character in a possible world wherein the author composed slightly differently, the author would be picking out a different kind that has different properties within it essentially. It is thus a consequence of this view that, if Gogol wrote *Dead Souls* slightly differently, so that the character called "Chichikov" were ascribed slightly different properties, Gogol would not have made Chichikov somewhat differently, instead he would have written about a different character entirely, for he would have delineated a different person-kind – one requiring different attributes of anyone who is an example of that kind (148).

But as Wolterstorff admits, this runs counter to our intuitions that

Surely Gogol could have developed the character Chichikov differently – more expansively, less expansively, in alternative ways. It's not just that he could have written a different text, with a world whose maximal component having the property of being called 'Chichikov' essential within it was different. He could have represented, or portrayed, Chichikov differently. So, too, having written one book, Conan Doyle offered the *further* adventures of Sherlock Holmes. And then there is the related phenomenon of different writers telling the story of Hercules, of Don Juan, of Faust – telling it differently (148).

To provide a sense in which it is true that Gogol could have written differently about Chichikov, Doyle wrote all of the stories about the same Sherlock Holmes, and Faust appears in works by Goethe and Marlowe, Wolterstorff begins by isolating the so-called components of a story (the kinds *carriage, yellow carriage,* etc.). These components each have "logical parts" – roughly those kinds that have essential within them a subset of the properties essential within the component (e.g., *carriage* is a logical part of *yellow carriage*). One can then distinguish the "maximal components" of stories (those components of stories that are not themselves logical parts of components) from mere components. Characters then are identified with maximal components of stories.

Let us see how this should help identify characters across literary works. Consider the problem of how to provide a sense in which the statement "Faust appears in works by both Marlowe and Goethe" is true. First, we must admittedly distinguish the Faust of Goethe's *Faust* from the Faust of Marlowe's *Dr. Faustus*, and so forth. But we can also speak of a certain character (person-kind) that has been picked out by those in the Western literary tradition, exhibiting only the "core" properties of each of the Faust characters. Wolterstorff calls this simply "the Faust character," having essentially within it merely such properties as being called "Faust," striking a pact with the devil, and so on (149). The Faust character is said to be a component of Goethe's *Faust*, but not a maximal component. The relevant maximal component is the Faust in Goethe's *Faust*, which has the Faust character as its logical part. So, the Faust in Goethe's *Faust* has essentially within it all of the properties essentially within the Faust character, but not vice-versa, and so can be said to "include" the latter character. The same can be said of the Faust in Marlowe's *Dr. Faustus*. Thus, although Goethe's Faust and Marlowe's Faust are not identical, one and the same Faust character appears in Goethe's *Faust* and in Marlowe's *Dr. Faustus* and is a logical part of each of the expanded characters. On this basis, we can legitimately say that there is a single Faust character that appears in each work. Each Faust in a particular literary work is a certain expansion of the basic Faust character, so the diverse works may be said to concern the same character, even though the complete character of each (Goethe's Faust, Marlowe's Faust) is different.

Wolterstorff's solution relies on the idea that in those cases in which characters from different literary works are rightly said to be identical we may distinguish some core set of properties that distinguish that character and then identify the basic character with the kind that has only these properties essential within it (and so appears as a component of each of the expanded characters). What, then, might count as such core properties? In Wolterstorff's example of Faust, he cites such core properties as striking a pact with the devil, being called "Faust," and so on (149). But could I not write a literary work in which Faust, in a less ambitious moment, decides *not* to make the pact with the devil and settles down to the quiet life of slow scientific inquiry? Surely it seems I could. So what are the relevant core properties? Even being called "Faust" seems inessential: I could write another play about a man very like Faust and call him "Phaust" but still be speaking of the same character. Just being a man? Then we fall into unacceptable conclusion that all literary works about men – works about Holmes, Hamlet, Faust, and so forth – are really just expansions talking about one and the same basic character.

In short, the view that fictional characters are to be identified by pointing towards the basic character's having essential within it merely a central core of properties faces a thorny dilemma. If one includes too many properties, one rules out a priori many plausible works about the same character (e.g., in which Faust refuses the devil). If one includes too few properties (e.g., being a man, being intelligent), one identifies works as being about the same basic character although in fact they are about wildly differing characters.

One might try to resolve this problem by simply making the condition fuzzier: Instead of specifying a set of core properties, one might only require that some fair number of a common pool of central properties be essential within both characters in order to call them "the same." This requires giving up the idea that there is one basic character appearing in each Faust work (because, on this view, characters are person-kinds that are identical only if they have exactly the same properties essential within them). But one might nonetheless say that there is a sense in which characters of different literary works are the same if they have this substantial overlap of properties, bearing rather a family resemblance to one another. But this still identifies characters that should not be identified, and separates characters that belong together. Characters can be very similar without being the same: If we pull out a core of properties, many of which must be shared for characters to be the same, we will end up identifying all of P. G. Wodehouse's well-heeled but silly upper-class bachelors, conniving social-climbing young ladies, and old interfering aunts. At the same time, if we are to get a reasonably large core of properties to prevent unwanted identifications, it seems we have to distinguish characters that change or develop greatly over the course of a series of works, for they

60

Agatha Christie — all the same genre

may have less in common with themselves than Wodehouse's bachelors have with each other.

Reicher offers a second attempt to identify characters across different sequels: Rather than finding the smallest character in common across the literary works, this solution is based on looking instead to the largest "total character" (*gesamtfigur*) in the work made up of all of the sequels.[7] She suggests that we can either count Sherlock Holmes as the one character encoding all of the properties ascribed to him in all of the stories taken together, or we may speak of many different Holmeses, each the Holmes of a particular work. Reicher admits that, in virtue of the fact that each of these encodes a different set of properties, no Holmes of one work is identical with a Holmes of another work, nor is any such Holmes of one work identical with the Holmes of the whole series. But suppose we treat the whole series of literary works as a single literary work and speak only of the Holmes of the whole work (joined up out of what we normally take to be distinct literary works). Then, the Holmes of each partial work is a logical part of the Holmes of the whole series, and we can reasonably speak of the whole Holmes as appearing (in part) in each of the partial stories.

A problem arises here: On what basis is a literary work to be counted as part of the same series as another work? Clearly we need good criteria for whether or not different works are to be united as sequels and counted as a single "whole" series. Otherwise I could equally well set together *Hamlet, Tom Sawyer,* and *A Study in Scarlet* and count Hamlet, Tom, and Holmes as being the same character in virtue of all forming parts of the same total character. Note that one cannot rule out such combinations merely by stipulating that the total character cannot encode contradictory properties (being a Dane and being an Englishman), for often one and the same character is ascribed contradictory properties in works that are genuinely part of the same series, as Watson is in the Holmes stories. Clearly Reicher would not want to count Hamlet, Tom, and Holmes all as parts of the same total character, and to be fair, clearly these literary works are not sequels to one another. Nonetheless, this points to the urgent need, if this suggestion is to go anywhere, for conditions under which we can say that one literary work is a sequel to another.[8]

What conditions might these be? On pain of circularity, it cannot be that the works be about the same character or characters. On the other hand, if one specifies that they must be about similar characters, as discussed previously, we get the wrong identifications, for sequels can be about a character who is very different across the two works, and works can be about very similar characters without either being a sequel to the other.

What conditions might work better? A rather obvious criterion is that, in order to be writing a sequel, the author of the second work must be familiar with the first work (first or second hand) and intend to be writing about the same characters. This certainly seems to be why we are so comfortable speaking of sequels by the same author (for who is more familiar with the original characters than their author?). It also explains why are willing to count as sequels literary works written later by someone familiar with the original work and attempting to describe other events relating to the same characters, and why we do not count literary works about similar characters as sequels to one another if they are merely similar by coincidence.

Although such conditions for sequels may be more accurate to our practices of identifying and distinguishing characters, they involve going beyond the basic principle of the abstractist position: That identity conditions can be offered on the sole basis of properties encoded by characters. For they require us to bring an historical element into the identity conditions for characters across texts: They must appear in texts historically and intentionally related to one another in the relevant way, via the later author's acquaintance with and intentions regarding the first character.

If we have no adequate criteria for what is to count as a sequel, this latter method of character identification is useless. But if we need to bring in a condition such as that in the preceding paragraph to properly explicate the notion of a sequel (and I see no obvious way around it), then that is simply a way of bringing the necessary historical condition for character identity in through the back door. Although we might get satisfying identity conditions on that basis, we can do so only at the cost of abandoning the basic abstractist position that only a character's (encoded) properties are relevant for its identity.

The moral here should be plain: Similar characters do not the same characters make (nor do dissimilar characters different characters make). This problem plagues all attempts to identify and distinguish characters solely in terms of the properties they have or encode, regardless of whether one requires them to have all the same properties, some identical subset of properties, the same essential properties, or merely a quorum of identical properties. Instead of treating them as ideal abstracta distinguished solely by their properties, we may get farther by treating fictional characters as historical entities individuated at least in part by the circumstances of their creation.

We can come far closer to capturing our ordinary practices in treating fictional characters as the same or different by treating fictional objects as dependent entities. The idea behind the resulting view of character identity is that we can track the identity of fictional characters and other dependent objects by tracking the preservation of their bases. Although we cannot offer a strict set of necessary and sufficient identity conditions, by using as criteria the conditions under which the necessary foundations of fictional characters are preserved we can offer identity conditions at least as clear as those we have for ordinary objects. For we also lack a finite set of necessary and sufficient identity conditions for middle-sized spatiotemporal objects; instead several merely necessary conditions (such as spatiotemporal continuity or sameness of species) or one infinite sufficient condition (having all of the same properties at the same times) are often offered.

There are two main tasks in offering identity conditions for fictional characters: Offering conditions within a literary work, and offering conditions across different literary works. I begin with the easier task of offering a finite set of sufficient (but not necessary) conditions for the identity of characters within a literary work and proceed to offer one necessary (but not sufficient) condition for the identity of fictional characters across literary works. The necessary condition provides grounds for determining whether characters across novels are identical or separate, and to adjudicate many straightforward cases of putative identity, so that even if entities do not fulfill our rigid set of sufficient conditions, we can sensibly apply the concepts of identity and difference to them.

Fulfilling the following two conditions is sufficient for fictional characters x and y to be identical:[9]

1. x and y appear in the same literary work.
2. x and y are ascribed exactly the same properties in the literary work.

Appearing in a literary work can be understood roughly as: A character appears in some literary work just in case it is ascribed some property in that work.[10] We require that x and y are ascribed exactly the same properties only so that we can distinguish different characters that appear in the same literary work, keeping Gudrun and Ursula, Rosencrantz and Guildenstern distinct. Although these are not necessary conditions, they allow us to justify some of our most central claims about character identity, for example that different readers of *Northanger Abbey* can both read about the same Catherine Morland, and that Dr. Jeckyll is Mr. Hyde.

The requirement that characters appear in the *same* literary work obviously presupposes identity conditions for literary works, which is not surprising given the immediate dependence of characters on the works in which they appear. Fleshing out these conditions for characters requires that we step back to investigate the identity conditions for literary works. By doing so we not only lay the groundwork for these identity conditions for fictional characters but also provide an example of how in general identity conditions for dependent abstracta may be drawn out without reducing these identity conditions to those of ordinary spatiotemporal entities or ideal abstracta.

To offer strict sufficient conditions for two books to count as copies of the same literary work, I begin by making a three-way terminological distinction among texts, compositions, and literary works. The choice of these terms is somewhat arbitrary but seems to correspond as closely as any such division would to the features discerned. By "text" I mean a sequence of symbols in a language (or languages); by "composition" I mean roughly the text as created by a certain author in certain historical circumstances; by "literary work" I mean roughly the novel, poem, short story, or so forth having certain aesthetic and artistic qualities and ordinarily telling a tale concerning various characters and events. For each of these we can speak of the abstract text type, composition, or literary work, as well as of particular tokens, copies or instances of texts, compositions, or literary works. The terminology becomes clearer in the definitions that follow.

Two books that have all of the same type of symbols in the same order as each other are of the same text type.[11] Nonetheless, books of the same text type may fail to be copies of the same composition. If, for example, by mere coincidence two authors compose identically worded tales, we may have books of the same text type, but two different compositions.

Because instances of compositions are propagated through copying texts and the identity of a composition relies on its being appropriately derived from an origin, to devise sufficient conditions for text instances to count as copies of the same composition we must find a way to ensure that the relevant relation to the origin is preserved down the chains of copying. For one text token to count as a (perfect) direct copy of another, it must both be directly causally connected to the first and be of the same text type. But we want to include not only direct (first folio) copies of an original as copies of the original composition, but copies of those copies, and so on. We can include copies all the way down the chain by defining "copy of" recursively as follows, where x, y and z are text tokens: x is a copy of y if x is a direct copy of y or, for some z, x is a copy of z and z is a copy of y. So for a text token x to be a copy of a text token y, x must be the product of such a chain of text copying that reaches back to y.[12]

But for two text tokens x and y to be copies of the same composition, they need not be part of the same chain of copying. Suppose I make two copies of *Hamlet*, call them a and b, and then make a copy of a and a copy of b and call them x and y respectively. According to the above criteria, x is not a copy of y, nor is y a copy of x, but nonetheless we want to say that they are instances of the same composition. More than one chain of copying can originate from the same origin, and x and y can be copies of the same composition even if they come from different copying chains, provided these have a common origin. Put more formally, x and y are instances of the same composition if and only if x is y, or x is a copy of y, or y is a copy of x, or for some text token z, x is a copy of z and y is a copy of z. This allows that the chains of copying may branch off from the origin in different directions, and that text tokens may be copies of the same composition in virtue of being appropriately derived from a common origin even if their paths of derivation are distinct.

Even though being appropriately derived in this way suffices to make x and y instances of the same composition, however, it is not sufficient for x and y to be instances of the same literary work. For literary works are not mere strings of symbols but rather require a certain community of individuals with the right language capabilities and background assumptions to read and understand the literary work. One and the same composition can serve as the foundation for two different literary works in the context of different readerships. An extreme example can perhaps make the point best: It is certainly at least thinkable that there be two languages, English and Twenglish, which have all of the same symbol types ("a," "b," "c," and the rest), and the same syntax, but in which different meanings attach to the same strings of symbols. In such a case, there could be two completely different works (inhabited by completely different characters, exhibiting different aesthetic and artistic properties) on the basis of the same text, one of which depends on competent users of English, the other on users of Twenglish (imagine, if you like, that the author is bilingual). The same can occur in cases in which there are not two different languages but merely two cultures so different that, although both would understand a literary work, they would understand different stories on the basis of the same text. This, for example, is how allegories and parodies work in times of censorship: One and the same composition may provide a pleasant animal tale for children, a political critique and call to insurrection for the rebels.

Nonetheless, we do not need to require that readers have exactly the same background assumptions in order to read the same literary work. If I am reading *Pride and Prejudice* my background assumptions about the current state of world fisheries or the depletion of the ozone layer are entirely irrelevant and so could differ dramatically from those of another reader without entailing that we read different literary works on the basis of the same words. We can take the role of the readership on which a literary work depends into account and lay out sufficient conditions for the identity of a literary work as follows: If x and y are instances of the same composition and also demand the same background assumptions and language capacities of readers, they are instances of the same literary work.[13] Any background assumptions not "demanded" by either text – such as those about the ozone layer – may vary among readers without interfering with their ability to be competent readers of the same literary work. By plugging this into the conditions given here for the identity of a character, we can get a more complete picture of these sufficient conditions for character identity.

As mentioned in previous paragraphs, these conditions confirm many of the central cases of identity about which we care for fictional characters, entailing, for example, that if two contemporary readers of English pick up different (but perfect) copies of *Northanger Abbey*, they can both think about the same character Catherine Morland and enter into a genuine discussion of what that (one) character is like. They can similarly ensure the truth of claims such as "Dr. Jeckyll is Mr. Hyde." For, by virtue of some identity claim in the work to the effect that Dr. Jeckyll and Mr. Hyde are identical, Dr. Jeckyll is thereby ascribed all of the properties previously ascribed to Mr. Hyde, and vice-versa, so that they thereby are ascribed all of the same properties in the relevant literary work. These conditions do *not*, however, entail that Fred Jones's Pamela and Richardson's Pamela are one and the same character. Because on account of the different origins of the two tales, these characters do not appear in the same composition, and hence are not in the same literary work, we need not conclude that they are identical, even if they are ascribed all of the same properties. Of course Richardson's and Fielding's Pamelas belong to different literary works as well, so both of these cases remain open so far, as both are cases in which character identity across literary works is at issue.

necessary across works, sufficient within works

IDENTITY CONDITIONS ACROSS LITERARY WORKS

Although the previous section provides sufficient conditions for character identity, they are not necessary. Most often the cases of character identity we discuss are those that span different texts. In fact, it is quite important to understanding our literary traditions to recognize how a single character like Sherlock Holmes may reappear in many different works of the same series, or a character like Gudrun may develop over the course of different D. H. Lawrence novels. Similarly, many literary works would not be comprehensible at all if we could not take them to include the well-known characters of other works. Stoppard's *Rosencrantz and Guildenstern are Dead* makes little sense if we do not see that these are the same Rosencrantz and Guildenstern from *Hamlet*, and Fielding's *Joseph Andrews* would lose much of its humor were he inventing a new young maid rather than poking fun at the character of Richardson's invention. In such cases we can reasonably claim that characters are identical even though they appear in different works or in different translations or editions of the same literary work. Thus we also need to offer identity conditions for characters across literary works.[14]

The prospects seem dim for drawing out a definitive set of necessary and sufficient conditions for character identity. But that does not place us in any worse a position than we already face in the case of formulating identity conditions for actual humans. We can at least specify an important necessary condition C for the identity of characters x and y appearing in literary works K and L respectively: The author of L must be competently acquainted with x of K and intend to import x into L as y.[15] By "competent acquaintance" I mean the kind of acquaintance that would enable the author to be a competent user of the name of x (supposing x were named), as it is used in K. This sets up (on our prior analysis of the reference of fictional names) a necessary condition for the author of L to be referring to x in L (and ascribing new properties to x). If the author is referring to x, x may be ascribed new properties in the new context of literary work L, in which case x appears as a character, y, of L. Although this criterion should not strictly be considered sufficient, it should (combined with sensible and careful textual analysis) provide a very good benchmark for whether or not we can reasonably claim that two characters are the same.

If characters fulfill this condition, then we have good grounds for claiming that x is y. For example, as author of *The Rainbow*, D. H. Lawrence was competently acquainted with the Gudrun of *The Rainbow* and, given the similarity of this character to the later character of *Women in Love*,

67

it seems that the Gudrun of *The Rainbow* and the Gudrun of *Women in Love* are intended as the same. Similarly, we have good reason to believe (given the close textual similarity of the two plays, and the playfulness with the form of drama itself manifested in the work) that Stoppard is competently acquainted with the Guildenstern of *Hamlet* and abundantly familiar with the original text, and also given the importance of identifying his characters with Shakespeare's to the subtlety and humor of his work, we have good reason to believe that Stoppard intends to import Guildenstern and his cohorts into *Rosencrantz and Guildenstern are Dead*. If this is so, we have good grounds for saying that the one Guildenstern appears in both dramas. Finally, we can say on this basis that Fielding's Pamela is Richardson's Pamela, but Fred Jones's Pamela is not. For Fielding was intimately enough acquainted with the first tale to offer a detailed parody of it and clearly intends to be ridiculing the earlier work and importing its characters for his own purposes. By contrast (by stipulation) Fred knew nothing of the earlier Pamela and did not intend to import her into his literary work, so his Pamela and Richardson's fail this necessary condition and cannot be the same character.

Often if, despite the fact that the above condition is fulfilled, we deny that a character of a sequel is identical to the original, what we really mean might be best interpreted as a denial not that they are the same character but rather that any *real* person would act at one time as described in the earlier literary work, at another time as described in the second work. Such complaints are often made about the Scarlett O'Hara of Alexandra Ripley's sequel to *Gone With the Wind* and seem best read as complaints about the author's violation of verisimilitude (in particular of laws of psychology), rather than denials of identity. Indeed, it is precisely the implicit identification to the two characters that makes readers of the second novel dissatisfied with the (failed) attempt at verisimilitude.

The possibility of unintentional reference shifts is what makes this merely a necessary, not sufficient, condition. It is possible that, even if the second author uses the name of x, a reference shift has occurred, so that the second author is no longer genuinely referring to the earlier character and ascribing it new properties, but rather (perhaps unbeknownst to herself) devising a new character of her own making. If, for example, a rock, dog, or town appears in a literary work and is called "Sherlock Holmes," but without that reference playing any role in constituting the character or the plot, it seems that (regardless of any intention), the author has only succeeded in naming a new character by an old name, not in ascribing new properties to the old Holmes. There may admittedly be fuzziness in certain cases, in which it is simply unclear whether the author of the second text (even given the relevant intentions) is saying outlandish things about an old character or inventing a new character (perhaps with an old name), and in which we are not even sure what would resolve the issue. Our speech practices even incorporate this vagueness, as we commonly speak of one character being "based on" another character or on a real individual, affirming some association weaker than identity. But weaker associations than strict identity are also necessary to track the cases of real individuals like people who change drastically, or daffodils that return year after year, but perhaps not as identical. Such associations are sometimes labeled cases of "survival" rather than strict identity, and these have a role in fiction as elsewhere.[16]

But the presence of some fuzzy cases in which any decision seems arbitrary do not mean that the concept of identity is inapplicable to fictional characters. Fuzzy cases similarly afflict attempts to offer identity conditions for real individuals, not only persons, but even more so plants, ships, fungi, and piles of rubbish. Such fuzziness with respect to identity is certainly not unique to fictional characters, and few would argue against allowing plants and fungi in our ontology on the basis of their tricky individuation. Again the troubles with fictional characters are not unique.[17]

What is significant is that criteria have been developed (based on the above theory about the dependencies of fictional characters and the reference of fictional names) that offer rigid sufficient conditions for identity, as well as a necessary condition for identity that should provide a means of deciding most cases of putative identity and of meaningfully saying that fictional characters are "identical with themselves and distinct from one another." There are many clear cases in which characters are identical, as well as many clear cases in which they are not, and we have some means to adjudicate difficult cases. Most importantly, the identity conditions offered here also resolve problems of identity in ways that correspond to our ordinary practices in judging fictional characters to be the same or different. This sets them apart from those that reduce the identity conditions of fictional characters to those of ideal entities and establishes one further advantage of treating fictional characters as dependent abstracta. Moreover, it shows the means for drawing out identity conditions for dependent entities of all types, whether or not they are concrete, by keeping track of whether or not their connections to their supporting entities are preserved.

Part Two

Ontological Decisions

Foreword

In Part One I argue that we should consider fictional characters not to be the strange occupants of another realm but rather as abstract cultural artifacts as ordinary as the works of literature in which they appear. If we do so, then the problems that arise for fictional characters, including how to refer to them and offer identity conditions for them, parallel problems for other abstract entities and cultural artifacts. I have attempted to show how these problems may be overcome by considering fictional characters to be dependent entities, thus removing two major stumbling blocks to postulating fictional characters and suggesting ways to overcome these problems for other dependent abstracta. But so far this merely eliminates reasons *not* to postulate fictional characters and does not provide us with any positive reason to postulate them.

It is now time to face the second question: Should we admit fictional characters into our ontology? The case of fictional characters provides occasion for reexamining the larger issue: What, in general, should we admit to our ontology, and on what grounds? One of the points of philosophy in general, and ontology more particularly, is to help us make sense of our world. Thus one goal in choosing an ontology is to select one that provides an adequate basis for understanding our experience of and discourse about the world. Naturally this does not mean that we can never determine that experiences are misleading, discourse fallacious, or practice in need of revision. It only requires that we seek a theory able to analyze what our experience is about and whether our sentences are true or false as consistently, adequately, and elegantly as possible overall.

Too often such common sense standards of theory construction are overlooked in the flashier game of seeing who can "make do" with the most minimal ontology. Instead of weighing costs and benefits of

73

admitting entities such as fictional objects, elimination is sought at all costs. Instead of assessing theoretic adequacy and ontological parsimony against the backdrop of a large-scale metaphysical picture, each decision is made piecemeal. I propose here to return to a slower method of investigation and, using fictional characters as a hotly disputed case in point, to try to weigh costs and benefits thoroughly in the context of a large-scale ontological picture before determining whether, all things considered, one can offer a better theory by postulating or eliminating fictional objects.

I thus begin by assessing the relative adequacy of theories of experience and discourse that do and do not postulate fictional objects. Theories of intentionality and of language alike have sought to avoid postulating fictional characters by treating such experiences and sentences as entirely lacking reference to an object. I argue, however, that such attempts to avoid reference to fictional characters not only interfere with our ability to make sense of central beliefs and practices about fiction but also lead to inferior theories of intentionality and language. Nonpostulating theories of intentionality are left unable to account for the copresence of certain defining features of intentionality; theories of language are left in a process of endless ad hoc tinkering instead of providing uniform and systematic analyses of sentences based purely on their logical form. Thus the desire to offer more elegant and adequate and less ad hoc theories of intentionality and language provides a strong initial motivation to postulate fictional objects. But I take it only as initial motivation, not as the final word. For the central motivation not to postulate fictional objects lies in considerations of ontological parsimony.

I thus turn next to assessing the costs and benefits of admitting fictional objects into our ontology. This requires an initial investigation into how one should make decisions about what to admit into one's ontology. Clear, thorough, and consistent ontological decisions need to be made against the background of a categorial ontology: A set of exhaustive, fine-grained, and relevant categories in which things might be claimed to exist. In Chapter 8 I tackle this first ontological task by using the fundamental investigations into dependence to draw out a system of ontological categories. This system of categories not only provides the conceptual space against which to develop a comprehensive and systematic view of what there is but also enables us to compare competing ontologies, to see new resolutions to old ontological difficulties, and to make systematic and consistent decisions about whether or not to admit entities of a particular kind, such as fictional objects, into our ontology.

Making decisions against the background of a system of categories brings to light the difference between genuine and false parsimony. Parsimony is a philosophical concept too often invoked and too little examined. The appeal to parsimony may be the most persistent motivation to reject fictional characters; thus our study of fiction provides the occasion to examine the concept of ontological parsimony, to distinguish what makes a theory genuinely parsimonious and when the parsimony supposed to be gained by eliminating certain entities is a sham. Many ontological mistakes might be avoided by carefully bearing in mind the distinction between genuine and false parsimony. It turns out that one such mistake is eliminating fictional characters in favor of literary works.

In the final chapter I turn to offer an appraisal of what there is. Inadequate categorial systems based on bifurcations like the real and the ideal, the material and the mental, lead to the systematic exclusion or misconstrual of certain types of entities, such as fictional objects, works of art, and social and cultural objects of all types. These problems suggest the need for a broader and more varied ontological picture. We can construct one from the relatively spare basis of spatiotemporal objects, mental states, and things dependent on them in various ways. This enables us to account for a far wider range of objects than those usually admitted, and in particular to offer a better analysis of cultural entities and dependent abstracta within the context of a systematic framework. The closing chapter describes this unified picture and how it can provide a better view of the variety of entities in the world around us.

6

Fiction and Experience

The task of a theory of intentionality is to offer an analysis of the directedness of our thoughts and experiences towards those objects in the world that they are about. Theories of intentionality, like those of language, have often been directed by a desire to avoid postulating fictional entities and have sought alternatives to Meinongian theories of intentionality just as Russell sought an alternative to a Meinongian theory of reference. The main line of devising a theory of intentionality that avoids fictional objects is the content approach, which was first formulated in modern terms by Husserl and is defended in a number of contemporary theories of intentionality, including those of Searle, Smith, and McIntyre.[1]

According to content theories, ordinary intentional relations to objects of our veridical perceptions can be analyzed into three basic parts: The conscious act, the object, and the content. The conscious act is the particular perceiving, thinking, wishing, or so forth that occurs at a particular place and time. The object of the intentional relation is the thing the perception, thought, or so forth is of or about, normally just an ordinary physical individual or state of affairs that is chanced upon by the intentional act. The content of an act plays a role analogous to Fregean senses; it is what picks out, or prescribes, the object of the intentional act; it is dependent upon the subject's conception of, and angle of perception of, the object, but it is normally not something of which the subject is explicitly aware during the intentional experience. In particular, the content is not the object of the intentional act.

This simple act-content-object structure of intentional relations has provided content theories with an apparently easy way to avoid having to postulate fictional characters. Acts that apparently concern fictional characters, it is said, are acts that have a content but no object. So if

I think of Sherlock Holmes, my thought may have a content such as ⟨the clever detective who lives on Baker Street⟩,[2] but that content fails to prescribe any object, just as, on a Fregean analysis of language, the description "the clever detective who lives on Baker Street" may have a sense but no referent. As Searle writes:

> The fact that our statements may fail to be true because of reference failure no longer inclines us to suppose that we must erect a Meinongian entity for such statements to be about. We realize that they have a propositional content which nothing satisfies, and in that sense they are not "about" anything. But in exactly the same way I am suggesting that the fact that our Intentional states may fail to be satisfied because there is no object referred to by their content should no longer puzzle us to the point where we feel inclined to erect an intermediate Meinongian entity or Intentional object for them to be about... there is no object which they are about.[3]

Theories of intentionality that refrain from postulating fictional objects often claim this avoidance of fictional objects as a substantial advantage.[4] Although it may seem to offer the route to a more parsimonious ontology, however, does treating our apparent experiences of fictional characters as "objectless" acts really provide the basis for a better theory of intentionality? I argue that it does not: Accounting for features of our experience of fictional objects poses enormous difficulties for theories of intentionality that refrain from postulating fictional objects.

PURE CONTENT THEORIES AND FICTION

One of the major tasks of a theory of intentionality is to offer the grounds for understanding some of the distinctive features of intentionality, including its so-called existence independence (the purported fact that intentional acts need not be directed at any existent object), its conception dependence (the fact that one and the same object may be picked out by two different intentional acts conceiving of it in two very different ways), and its context sensitivity (the fact that two internally indistinguishable intentional acts may pick out different objects in different contexts).[5]

The content is, for the content theorist, not only the defining feature of intentionality but also the key to explaining the distinctive features of intentionality. And indeed the content theory can do very well at explaining the distinctive features of intentionality – as long as it is permitted to do so one feature at a time. For example, as mentioned previously, the content theorist analyzes the feature that the object of the intentional act need not exist by allowing that an intentional act can have a content that simply fails to prescribe any object whatsoever. The fact that the intentional relation changes according to the subject's conception of the object can be explained by the fact that two or more contents can prescribe one and the same object, so there is no problem in saying that quite different acts with distinct contents may be directed towards the same entity. The content theorist can similarly explain how one and the same mental conception or thought can pick out two different objects, for in different circumstances two instantiations of the same ideal content can pick out different objects in the world – different pennies that appear identical in perception, or different liquids that are conceived of on earth and twin-earth alike under the content ⟨water⟩.[6]

By such means the content theory can easily account for most of the major characteristics of intentionality, taken individually. Yet it is not enough for a theory to account for the singular occurrence of each feature of intentionality, for the features of intentionality can also occur together. In particular, intentional acts purportedly lacking an existent object may also exhibit conception dependence and context sensitivity, just as our veridical perceptual acts do. It is in analyzing such features of our experience of fictional objects that the limitations of the content theory come to the surface. Content theories of intentionality have typically avoided facing up to these problems by considering as examples of acts "not directed toward any existent object" such marginal and unusual cases as seeing a centaur, rather than offering analyses of the far more complex and important experiences of fiction. Analyzing our intentional relations to fictional objects should be one of the most important tests of a theory of intentionality because they provide what should be the central cases of intentional acts that purportedly lack reference to any existent object, and because we have such a wealth of experiences of fictional objects of which we need to make sense.

One difficulty in treating experiences of fictional characters as "objectless acts" arises in explaining the directed, relation-like character of intentionality. Intentionality certainly seems a classic example of a relation, namely that between consciousness and its objects. The characterization of intentionality as a relation enables us both to explain its directed character (as a nonsymmetric relation between something that is pointing and that towards which it is pointing) and to explain how it is that the real world and consciousness interact in perceptual acts (as the two terms of a certain kind of relation, mediated by a mental content).

The content theory maintains a minimal ontology by allowing that some intentional acts, including those directed towards fictional entities, lack an object entirely. Thus, if it is a relation at all, intentionality must either be conceived of as having the structure of a two-term relation between act and object, although it sometimes lacks a second (object) term; or as having the structure of a three-term relation among act, content, and object, although it sometimes lacks the third term.[7] So the content theory is forced to either give up the idea that intentionality is a relation (as Johansson does),[8] or to postulate a strange, possibly incoherent kind of relation simply to account for intentionality. In either case, the account it can give of the directedness of intentionality is limited to its being a directedness through a content, which is sometimes a directedness towards nothing at all.[9]

Regardless, however, of whether one is, or can be made, comfortable with the idea that intentionality is not a relation or is a variable-term relation (sometimes with three terms, sometimes with two), the deeper problems arise for the content theory not in its characterization of the intentional relation but rather in its analyses of the other characteristics of intentionality. For, precisely because the content theorist treats experiences of fiction as objectless acts, its classic solutions to the conception dependence and context sensitivity of intentionality do not seem to work in the case of fictionally directed acts.

Conception Dependence

Two of the most important features of intentionality are that the act "need not have any existent object," and that the intentional relation is conception-dependent. A quick look at fictional characters should make it clear that there can be intentional acts for which, according to the content theory, there are no existing objects, but yet for which it seems that one object is conceived under two or more different concepts. Consider the following intentional acts:[10]

Case A: 1. My thought about the current President of the United States
           2. My thought about the father of Chelsea Clinton

and:

Case B: 3. My thought about King Lear
           4. My thought about the father of Cordelia

The content theory can analyze the fact that in case A we have two intentional acts, two conceptions, and one object, by explaining that these two acts have different contents, ⟨the current President of the United States⟩ and ⟨the father of Chelsea Clinton⟩, but these contents pick out one and the same object, namely Bill Clinton. Thus the content theory can explain how it is that I can have lots of different thoughts that all are about one and the same real person, conceived in different ways.

In the second case we want just as much to be able to say that the two acts are about the same object. The trouble with the latter pair of acts is that according to the content theory these also exhibit the first feature of intentionality: The object of these acts does not exist. So, in accord with the earlier analysis, the content theory simply reports that in case B there are two intentional acts with two different contents, but no object. So our ability to explain that these two thoughts are about the same thing, namely King Lear, is lost, for it seems that the content theory can only tell us that there is no object in either case.

It would be a deep failing of any theory of intentionality if it could not explain what made acts (1) and (2) about the same object. Such objections are in fact often brought up against the early theory of Brentano and even at times against Meinong. But these intentional acts are structurally parallel to acts (3) and (4), and it is just as much a part of our experience that (3) and (4) are about the same object; we could not even begin to read and understand a novel if we could not so unify our intentional acts with different contents as being about the same character. It is just as much a failing for an intentional theory to be unable to account for (3) and (4) being about the same thing as it is for such a theory to be unable to account for (1) and (2) being about the same thing.

Some may object to my way of speaking and maintain that the problem of how to say that (3) and (4) are about the same *thing* cannot arise precisely because they are about *no thing* whatsoever. I have used the turn of phrase "about the same thing" merely because it is how, colloquially, we would normally express the experience of two different thoughts about the same character, or about the same number or abstract object. So I do not mean by "thing" here a spatiotemporal individual object. I maintain, however, that regardless of the manner of speaking that is used, a problem persists for the content theorist, namely, how to unify (3) and (4).

The case can be made in a slightly different way if we consider another thought apparently about a fictional character, for example:

5. My thought about the famous playwright murdered by Humbert Humbert.

Not only does the content theory have no way of explaining that thoughts (3) and (4) are about the same thing; it seems to lack completely a way of saying that (3) and (4) have something in common that (5) does not have. It can tell us only that they all have different contents and all fail to have any object whatsoever. Even someone who adamantly wanted to resist all talk about fictional objects would need to find some way of explaining this unity that exists between (3) and (4) but not between (3) and (5). The content theory of intentionality, however, seems at first glance to give us no way of doing so.

One could keep in line with classical content theories by refusing to postulate anything as the object of experiences of fictional entities, and attempting nonetheless to explain why it is that the intentional acts (3) and (4) belong together in a way that (3) and (5) do not. One might reply that what unifies these acts is that they are all experienced by the judging subject or subjects *as if* they were of the same object: These acts include a phenomenological individuation of the object *for consciousness* although there is no external object and hence no metaphysical individuation of King Lear at all. In this case that would mean that thoughts (3) and (4) are unified in that they are presented as being about the same individual, namely King Lear, whereas thought (5) is presented as about a different individual, namely, Clare Quilty of Vladimir Nabokov's *Lolita*. This pushes the question back to: In virtue of what are thoughts (3) and (4) presented as being about the same individual but (5) is not?

Smith and McIntyre offer an account of phenomenological individuation for consciousness according to which "an object is *individuated in* an act or attitude insofar as the act's Sinn [content] either presupposes or explicitly includes (in some appropriate way) a sense of which individual a given thing is, a sense of its 'identity.' "[11] Normally, what is presupposed is a set of background beliefs about the principles of individuation for the kind of individual given, as well as beliefs that ascribe various identity-relevant properties to that individual. So what might make my thoughts about King Lear phenomenologically individuated would be first my set of background beliefs about what principles of individuation are relevant for humans, as well as a set of beliefs about King Lear. We might formulate a principle for grouping King Lear–type thoughts as:

T is a King Lear thought if and only if the content of T is such that it seems to prescribe a man the same as the king with two ungrateful daughters, who abdicates the throne early, dies heartbroken over Cordelia's body, and so forth.

These could serve both to unify my King Lear thoughts and to separate them from my Quilty thoughts, for my background principles of

81

individuation for humans might tell me that the man with the above properties cannot be the same as a twentieth-century American playwright who dies of gunshot wounds inflicted by a jealous pederast. This indeed takes us some way towards understanding the individuative consciousness of fictional characters but, I think, is not enough of itself. Unifying our thoughts about literary characters solely on the basis of their individuation in consciousness is both too narrow to unify all our same-character thoughts and too broad to keep some thoughts directed at two different characters from being treated as picking out the same character. The latter problem is, I think, the more formidable, but I treat them in turn.

First, the above account of individuation in consciousness of fictional objects treats their individuation as parasitic on the individuation in consciousness of real objects, for their phenomenological individuation relies, by hypothesis, on background beliefs about principles of individuation for real entities of the kind in question (so, for example, my phenomenological individuation of King Lear relied on my background beliefs about individuation conditions for humans). But fictional characters can and do wildly violate our real-world principles of identity for entities of the kind as which they are represented without thereby losing their identity. Our background beliefs about little girls might well tell us that no little girl is identical with a blueberry, yet in Roald Dahl's *Charlie and the Chocolate Factory* Violet Beauregard *is*, later in the story, a giant blueberry. Thus we need a way of explaining why it is that my initial thought ⟨that obstinate child will get her due⟩ is to be unified as a thought of the same Violet-type as my later thought ⟨that abnormally sized piece of fruit was sent to the juicing room⟩, even if I (or even all readers) perhaps omit to read the intermediate section of the book in which the transformation occurs, so that the element of sameness is not preserved in the contents of my respective acts and would seem to be excluded by my background beliefs.

Similarly, fictional works often describe whole new species of entities regarding which we have no background beliefs about individuation on which we can rely in individuating these entities for our consciousness. Objects can even be represented as changing ontological type or exhibiting contradictory properties. The unruliness of fictional characters, based on the fact that they may be ascribed properties that violate normal real-world individuative principles without thereby losing their identity, is probably a major reason for the oft-maintained view that fictional entities cannot be individuated at all.[12]

What this shows is not that fictional entities cannot be properly in-dividuated for consciousness, but rather that either their principles of individuation for consciousness have to be formulated differently than the phenomenological individuation of real individuals or the individ-uation of these objects cannot be identified with their individuation for consciousness. Given the unruliness of fictional characters, it seems highly unlikely that a mere admixture of beliefs about the individual and back-ground beliefs about individuative principles for the kind in question can be sufficient even for individuating these entities for consciousness, much less for properly grouping our various intentional acts that we need to explain as being about the same fictional object.

Solutions based in individuation *for consciousness* also are unable to cope with other cases in which it seems as if there are two or more experiences of the same object: If two different individuals both think of Hamlet, or if one individual does so over time without being aware of her or his earlier experience. Although in practice we treat it as being possible that such experiences be about the same thing, in cases such as these there may be no individual for whom these experiences are presented as being about one and the same object.

Context Sensitivity

The converse problem of intentionality, that one and the same mental conception can pick out two or more different objects, also applies to the apparent experience of fictional entities. As I argue in earlier chap-ters, fictional entities are created at a certain time by the acts of an author or authors and are rigidly tied to their origins, so that authors working independently, in separate traditions and working from inde-pendent sources, can at most create similar (not identical) characters. Thus, as I argue, if some Fred Jones purely coincidentally (without ac-quaintance with Richardson's or Fielding's work) wrote a play about a young maid called "Pamela," his Pamela must be a different character than Richardson's, at most remarkably similar to the original. And this is the case even if Jones happens by some extreme coincidence to write all of the same words, in the same order, as those in Richardson's tale.

Given this analysis of the identity conditions required for fictional characters, my single thought about Pamela the maid, with the single content ⟨Pamela the maid⟩, could pick out either Jones's or Richardson's Pamela. The content theory cannot distinguish the intentional act with the content ⟨Pamela the maid⟩ directed at Richardson's Pamela from

⟨Pamela the maid⟩ directed at Jones's Pamela. For because they both have the same content but no object, there is no way of differentiating them.

The problem of one content and two objects is more critical, as it suggests that the individuation of fictional objects cannot be identified with their phenomenological individuation regardless of how we analyze their phenomenological individuation. Suppose we accept the earlier suggestion that there are no fictional objects but that we can adequately explain what unifies our various thoughts that are as if they were about a single fictional object by appeal to the purported individuation of such entities in the contents of the thoughts about them. We can, however, have two acts with qualitatively identical contents – attributing the very same properties to the object, invoking the same background individuative principles and background beliefs about the properties of the object, and ascribing sameness to the objects in question – that are nonetheless about *different* fictional objects. In short, this solution provides no explanation of how it is that, even in our intentional relations to fictional entities, the same content (taken alone) may in different contexts prescribe two or more different objects.

For consider once again the twin-Pamela case, in which the character Pamela created by Fred Jones in 1957 is assigned all and only those properties assigned to the more famous Pamela. As long as a strict internalist content theory is maintained, providing the solution to the question of how we unify thoughts about the same fictional objects solely in terms of relations among the contents of those acts, we are forced to conclude that my thought on reading about Jones's Pamela is to be "about the same character" as my qualitatively identical thought about Richardson's Pamela. But this violates our practices in requiring an appropriate historical connection to the original character for a later character to count as identical with an earlier one.[13]

What this seems to show is that, even in the case of fictional characters, the identity of the object is transcendent in relation to any finite set of contents about that object – that there is some real metaphysical identity of fictional characters apart from their individuation for consciousness.[14] It also suggests that part of what this external identity of fictional characters relies on is the circumstances of their creation.

PURE CONTEXTUALIST THEORIES AND FICTION

Before concluding that we need to postulate fictional objects to offer an adequate theory of intentionality, it would be well to attempt a different solution that does not postulate fictional objects and yet does take into account the context of intentional acts directed towards them. Perhaps a contextualist solution to how to group intentional acts apparently directed at the same fictional object can succeed where internalist solutions fail. A different approach to the two-content, one-object problem that does not take recourse in postulating fictional objects might go outside the intentional relation entirely and instead track the apparent identity of fictional characters by means of a principle such as:

T is a King Lear thought if and only if the thinker of T is situated in an appropriate context before a copy of *King Lear* (causally derived from Shakespeare's original).

For example, that my two King Lear thoughts belong together while my Quilty thought does not belong with them, we might explain by referring to the fact that my King Lear thoughts occur in the same context – probably while seated before a single spatiotemporal object (a book) in which tokens of the appropriate words are written, which effect my eyes as I think these King Lear thoughts. My Quilty thought, however, probably occurs before different word-tokens instantiated in a different spatiotemporal object. If my copies of *Lolita* and *King Lear* happened to be reprinted in a single volume, this would be no objection, for each work has a distinct history as a separate whole; we need only to trace back the history of each part of the volume in my possession to different manuscripts in order to separate out the relevant historical contexts behind my King Lear thoughts and my Quilty thoughts.

Yet occurrence in this kind of contextual circumstance, before a book belonging to the appropriate historical chain of publication, may be necessary but would not be sufficient to unify sets of thoughts as being of "the same character," that is, to classify these as thoughts of the same type, for example as King Lear thought types. Critiques of pure contextualist views of perception, which have argued that the same external contextual relation can be maintained (including affecting the subject's eyes in certain ways) without a perception of the object occurring,[15] should have even more force in the case of fiction. The historical and current contextual relations between copies of *King Lear* and my conscious acts might be left intact, but we would not want to say that the relevant thoughts are King Lear–type thoughts. I could, for example, let my thoughts wander even while still reading, or simply fail to unify the relevant words into projecting the represented object, the father of Cordelia, or I could be attending to the changes in meter of:

> We'll no more meet, no more see one another.
> But yet thou art my flesh, my blood, my daughter –
> Or rather a disease that's in my flesh,
> Which I must needs call mine (*King Lear* II.4.221–224.)

In such a case the same perception of words is maintained, but the thought is not a King Lear–type thought but a thought about meter. Without recourse to content, and probably even to a prior notion of character identity, we cannot successfully group the thoughts about the same character together by means of historical or current context.

COMBINED CONTENT/CONTEXT APPROACH

A combined content/context approach to intentional acts apparently directed at fictional objects would seem to have a far greater chance than either pure internalist or externalist views at successfully grouping thoughts about fictional characters without postulating fictional objects. Whether we count a thought as a King Lear–type thought might then be formulated in the following principle:

T is a King Lear thought if and only if the thinker of T is situated in an appropriate context before a copy of *King Lear* (causally derived from Shakespeare's original) and the content of T is such that it seems to prescribe a man the same as the king with two ungrateful daughters, who abdicates the throne early, dies heartbroken over Cordelia's body, and so forth.

This gets us, I think, rather close to being able to classify the appropriate intentional acts as King Lear–type acts. Even the best combined account, however, still suffers from the problem of coincidence: There may still be cases in which I am appropriately contextually situated before a copy of *King Lear*, and in which I imagine a proud and foolish old king with three daughters, but in which this is merely coincidental. Perhaps I have never read the play and am merely checking the text for the number of occurrences of the letter *j*. Bored in this activity, I allow my mind to wander to my favorite royal fantasy. Although the content of my thought ⟨the old king with two ungrateful daughters⟩ is suitable and although I am situated in the appropriate context before a copy of *King Lear*, this should not be classed a genuine King Lear–type thought. Such thoughts would be analogous to a case in which I hallucinate a plate of goulash while

86

situated contextually before a real plate of goulash: Context and content are in place, but nonetheless the act is not *about* the relevant object; it is only coincidental that both conditions are fulfilled at the same time. Theories that refuse to postulate objects for our intentional acts apparently directed toward fictional objects cannot explain the connection between thought and object necessary to make this a genuine King Lear thought instead of a random thought coincidentally occurring in the appropriate context.

We might insist that the thought with the appropriate content not only occur in the relevant context but itself be caused by reading a copy of *King Lear*. This does not resolve the problem, however, for there are many ways in which reading the relevant copy of the text could serve as the causal basis for thoughts that are nonetheless not about Lear. Reading of Lear's approaching madness could trigger thoughts of my old friend Lars, now sadly lost to madness, and his long mad ravings about a remarkably (although only coincidentally) Lear-like king. Although reading the text is the cause of the Lear-like thought, the thought is still not a thought about King Lear, and so we remain subject to the coincidence problem, as we are unable to screen out irrelevant thoughts caused by reading the book before us.

All manner of cognitive links could provide devious causal connections from reading the book to thoughts that happen to have an appropriate content. The combination theorist does not merely have to assert that it is in virtue of *some* causal link to the appropriate text that the thought with the right content occurred but must attempt to distinguish "right" from "wrong" causal paths, counting only those thoughts caused by the "right" cognitive links as genuine Lear thoughts (instead of thoughts about the king of Lars's ravings). Yet even if the various causal paths from text to thought could be isolated, purely physical links of neurons do not come prelabeled as "right" and "wrong" for genuine Lear-thought causation. Moreover, one could not distinguish "right" from "wrong" causal paths merely descriptively, calling the "right" path that which most readers' brains followed, for it is certainly possible, however unlikely, that – thanks to some widespread quirk of brain wiring – the majority of readers would end up with non-Lear thoughts. Some normative judgment or interpretation is required to determine which causal paths are the right ones to cause genuine Lear thoughts and which are the wrong ones. There seems little hope of finding a basis for this judgment apart from in a prior notion of what should count as a Lear thought. But criteria for what should count as a Lear thought are precisely what the combined theory was supposed to provide: If the criteria invoked are those of a combined theory, we become involved in a vicious circle. Yet if the criteria are those of a pure content or context theory, then (if the above arguments are correct) they will result in mistakes about which thoughts are classified as Lear thoughts.

Thus it seems that to avoid the coincidence problem we have to go beyond the thought's content and causal history in order to explain what makes a thought a Lear-type thought – perhaps by postulating a fictional character that this thought is about. By doing so, one can offer a unilevel theory of intentionality, according to which every intentional act has both a content and an object, providing the means to account for the presence of the distinctive features of intentionality for experiences of all kinds of objects.

THE INTENTIONAL OBJECT THEORY OF INTENTIONALITY

Let the theory for which I shall argue be called the "intentional object theory" of intentionality. It is a theory based in the idea that all intentional acts have both a content and an object, which in no case may be identified with each other.[16] So unlike pure content theories, the intentional object theory maintains that there is always an object of the intentional act. In no case may the content and object of the presentation be identified with each other, for it is always possible for the same object to be picked out by two or more different contents. Moreover, it is at least in principle possible (for acts with some kinds of content) that the same content pick out two or more objects. These central features of intentionality are preserved as much in our conscious experiences of fictional objects and hallucinations as in our everyday perceptual experience. By postulating an object of fictionally directed intentional acts we can at last say, quite simply, what the various King Lear–type acts have in common: They, like the different Bill Clinton–type acts, are acts with different contents directed towards the same object (the fictional character King Lear and the person Bill Clinton, respectively).

Nonetheless, the object of the intentional act need not exist independently of intentional acts being directed towards it; indeed it may even be created in the act itself. In general, because according to the intentional object theory every intentional act has an object as well as a content, if there is no preexistent object that the thought is about, a mind-dependent intentional object is generated by that act. Thus hallucinations or imaginings, too, turn out to have objects which, typically, are created by that intentional act itself; they are quite literally figments or fabrications of the mind. These dependent objects are the so-called "purely intentional objects" discussed by Ingarden, which depend on intentionality for their very existence.[17] Fictional characters turn out to be a particularly interesting subclass of purely intentional objects.[18]

The basic structure of the intentional relation, according to the intentional object theory, is a nonsymmetric mediated relation between a conscious act and the object of which it is conscious. A relation R is nonsymmetric if aRb neither entails that bRa holds nor that it does not hold. Clearly from the relation that Ann thinks about Bob we can neither conclude that Bob thinks about nor does not think about Ann (as a matter of empirical fact, however, most relations of intentionality are asymmetric).

A mediated relation is one with two (or more) terms, A and B, between which the relation holds in virtue of a third entity C, such that if C changes so does the identity of the relation (and sometimes the kind of relation). Common examples of mediated relations are easy to find. The relation of brother-in-law is one such mediated relation, in which, for example, Bob is a brother-in-law of Ann if there is a person Calvin who is Ann's husband and Bob's brother. In this case, if Ann did not have this husband, then the relation between Ann and Bob would not exist. Nonetheless, as in the case of intentionality, it is possible for Ann to remain in the brother-in-law relation, mediated by Calvin, but related to a different object (just as, in intentionality, one content may prescribe two different objects). For example, if Calvin has two brothers, Bob and Bill, then the same kind of relation holds between Ann and Bill as between Ann and Bob, with the same mediator (Calvin). It is also possible to replace the mediator but maintain the same kind of relation between the two terms of the original relation via a different mediator. This, for example, could happen if Ann divorced Calvin and married brother-in-law Bob. In this case a brother-in-law relation would still exist between Ann and Bill, but via a different mediator. This case corresponds to the feature of intentionality that the same object can be intended through two or more contents.

Conceiving of intentionality as a mediated relation allows us to explain the facts that two contents may prescribe the same object, and that two objects may be prescribed by the same content. But we do so without having to abandon the idea that intentionality is essentially relational in character and without having to postulate some special new kind of relation that applies to intentionality alone. Moreover, if intentionality is a mediated relation, there is no need to postulate incomplete objects as the objects of our perceptual acts (as Meinong does) in order sufficiently to distinguish acts from each other.

The intentional object theory of intentionality explains the phenomenon that the objects of our intentional acts "need not exist" in part by rewriting this claim. The objects of our intentional acts need not be physical, spatiotemporal, or ideal entities, and they need not exist independently of intentional acts. This is because one term (the object term) may depend in a variety of ways on the other term (the intentional act) and may even (in the case of creative acts of fictionalizing or hallucinating) be brought into existence by that very intentional act. Thus in this view what is distinctive about intentionality is not that it is a relation that may lack a second term but rather that it is creative; whether in the case of ordinary performative speech acts or creative acts of imagination, an intentional act may bring its object into existence. Thus I would not say that the object of an intentional act need not exist, but only that it need not exist independent of human intentionality.

The object of an intentional act may be of several different types and may even be created by the intentional act itself. The object of an intentional relation may derive its existence from that intentional act, or it may be simply accessed (picked out) by that act, or it may stand in some intermediary relation of dependence to the act in question. For example, typically the object of a hallucinatory act is created by that act itself, whereas the object of a veridical perceptual act is just picked out by that intentional act, not created by it. The intentional relation varies in the kinds of dependence relations (if any) that obtain between the object and the intentional act.

The intentional object theory, combined with the above view of the structure of fictional objects, can explain the features of our intentional experiences of fictional objects (two contents, one object; one content, two objects; and the coincidence problem) that content, contextualist, and mixed theories could not. It can explain, for example, what my thoughts about the father of Goneril and about the father of Cordelia have in common by postulating the fictional entity King Lear, which both acts have as their common object although they involve conceiving of King Lear under different contents. The two-content, one-object phenomenon in the case of fiction then admits of precisely the same analysis as in the case of real objects.

The context sensitivity of intentionality can likewise now be given a parallel analysis for acts directed towards real and fictional individuals. The difference between my Pamela thought and my twin-Pamela thought, both conceived under the content ⟨Pamela the maid⟩, is that they concern distinct fictional objects. Thus, for example, when reading Richardson's *Pamela*, the object of my act is the Pamela of Richardson because the copy of the text that is causally related to my act is also causally derived in an appropriately preserved chain of publication derived from Richardson's original text. The same goes for a case of reading Jones's *Pamela*: In that case the thought is about the Pamela of his creation. In short, the thoughts are about different things even if the contents are identical, for in each case the thought is about the character founded in that very work of literature before me, yet these are distinct works of literature supporting distinct characters, one created by Richardson, the other independently created by Jones.

Postulating fictional characters as described here can also answer the coincidence challenge, which even the best solution that refrained from postulating fictional objects, the combined content/context approach, could not. Consider a case in which, while reading *King Lear*, I picture the aged king to myself.[19] What makes a thought a King Lear–type thought is being of or about the fictional character King Lear. I argue in Chapter 4 that reference to fictional characters need not be merely descriptive, because we can also refer to them rigidly via their textual foundations. Similarly, an intentional content prescribing a fictional character need not be (and typically is not) merely descriptive; it may contain an element of indexicality referring to this very character founded on this literary work before me.[20] Thus in a genuine case of fictionally seeing it is no mere coincidence that the content of my act prescribes some Lear-like king while I happen to be situated before a copy of *King Lear*. Quite the contrary, the content of my thought in this situation may contain an implicit indexical element such as ⟨this character that I am reading about right now . . . ⟩ and hence have a content that cannot be satisfied by any Lear-like imagining but only by the fictional character King Lear himself, founded on this very literary work of which I have a copy before me. This differs markedly from the case of coincidentally imagining a Lear-like king while situated before the work. For in the latter case the content (describing some coincidentally Lear-like king) does not prescribe this particular fictional character founded on this text at all, just as the content of an act of imagining some goulash may not prescribe the particular plate of goulash in front of the imaginer. Thus postulating intentionality-dependent fictional objects as the objects of some of our intentional acts can indeed answer the challenges posed of analyzing the interaction of the various features of intentionality in fictionally directed acts and indeed can offer parallel analyses of the features of intentionality regardless of whether these acts are directed towards ordinary or fictional entities.

Choosing a theory of intentionality, like choosing any theory, is a matter of weighing advantages and disadvantages concerning how well the theories can account for the data, what ontological or methodological complexity they require, what other phenomena they might be able to explain, and so on. The complex field of data provided by our intentional experiences of fictional entities has long been overlooked, despite the importance of fiction in daily human life, and although fiction should provide one of the most important test cases for a theory of intentionality. Content, contextualist, and mixed theories that shun the additional ontological complexity of fictional objects all, as we see, run into various difficulties in explaining features of our experience of fictional objects, and there seems no immediately promising means of resolving these difficulties.

The intentional object theory is proposed as a means of surmounting these difficulties through a uniform account of intentionality as a relation of act to object, mediated by a content. Its apparent disadvantage vis-à-vis the other mentioned theories is that, because the intentional object theory maintains that every intentional act has an object as well as a content, it must postulate more objects and more kinds of object than its occasionally objectless counterparts. We cannot finally evaluate the relative parsimoniousness of postulating and nonpostulating theories until after we have engaged in preliminary work on ontological categories and the nature of parsimony, issues to which I return in Chapters 8 and 9.

For now we can at least see one initial advantage of postulating fictional objects as conceived in Part I: So doing enables us to offer a better theory of intentionality. One advantage is that the intentional object theory conceives of intentionality as a proper relation. Content theories cannot do so precisely because they maintain that there are objectless acts, in which case there is only one term. This should be a prima facie advantage for the newer theory, for it gives us the ontological tools to account for the feature of intentionality cited above, that it is "relation-like" without having to postulate a strange one-term pseudorelation unique to intentionality. Most importantly, postulating dependent fictional characters as the objects of some intentional acts enables the intentional object theory to offer adequate analyses of the copresence of the features of intentionality in all kinds of intentional acts; those theories that avoid the ontology of fictional objects seem unable to do so.

7

Fiction and Language

Far more intensive work has been done on analyzing fictional discourse than fictional experience. As in the case of intentionality, most of this work has been done in pursuit of the idea that there really are no fictional objects to which we can refer and so has been driven by a desire to avoid reference to fictional objects at all costs. But again the issue properly should not be conceived as whether we can get away without referring to fictional characters, but rather as whether we can offer a better theory of language by occasionally admitting reference to fictional characters. I argue that we can.

Many problems in speaking of fictional characters parallel those for thinking of them. Sentences such as "all parties to the discussion are speaking of the same character" express the tacit assumptions behind all critical discourse about how to understand and interpret literary characters. It seems that attempts to understand such sentences without referring to fictional characters, whether by appealing to the senses involved, the context of reference, or some combination of these, would run into problems parallel to those described above. Yet giving up the idea that such sentences could be true in a robust sense (not just that they were alike in thinking of nothing at all) would be to give up a great deal.

But rather than rehashing those problems for the case of language, I wish to focus on the problem that brought discussion of fiction into analytic philosophy: How to analyze statements apparently referring to fictional characters. Fictional discourse was largely brought into discussion to provide examples of sentences involving nonreferring terms, to contrast with ordinary sentences involving referring terms. Rather than being argued for, it was simply presupposed at the start that such names did not refer, and that presupposition for the purpose of examples quickly became gospel. No doubt fictional names provided familiar and useful examples for the points about reference under discussion in those contexts. But does it stand up as an analysis of fictional discourse? Or could we offer a better theory of language by allowing for reference to fictional characters?

PARAPHRASE AND PRETENSE

In an effort to avoid fictional characters, philosophers of language dealing with fiction have often taken their task to be that of providing analyses of statements apparently about fictional objects that, despite the nonreference of fictional terms, yield truth-values that accord with our ordinary beliefs about which statements are true, and which false. Simple Russellian or Fregean analyses of sentences containing fictional names failed to meet the challenge, since they provided sentences involving fictional terms with truth-values at odds with our normal beliefs and practices about which sentences are true and which false. A straightforward Russellian analysis would evaluate all simple (unprefixed) statements about fictional characters such as "Hamlet is a prince" as false. For they would be read in the logical form of "There is some x such that x is Hamlet and x is a prince," while there is no such x. A straightforward Fregean view would evaluate all such statements as lacking truth-value: Since the fictional name fails to refer, the entire sentence containing it must also lack a reference to the True or the False and thus be truth-valueless. Since these simple analyses provide all simple sentences about fiction with the same truth-value, they do not preserve the distinction between correct claims about fictional characters such as "Hamlet is a prince" and "Hamlet was created by Shakespeare" and incorrect claims like "Hamlet is a frog" and "Hamlet was created by Ronald Reagan."

The standard means of facing these difficulties for the disbeliever in fictional objects lies in applying the paraphrase technique to rewrite sentences apparently about fictional objects in such a way that they no longer purport to refer to fictional objects, but nonetheless come out with the truth-value we would be pre-theoretically inclined to assign the paraphrased statement. Sophisticated nonpostulating views of fiction can satisfactorily analyze discourse about sequences of events and traits of characters as they are presented in stories by prefixing such statements with a story operator. For the Fregean, prefixing statements such as "Hamlet is a prince" with "according to the story" puts the original statement in an indirect context, so that the expanded statements can have a truth-value

94

regardless of the fact that the fictional name does not (normally) refer. For the Russellian, because in the expanded statement the fictional name has secondary occurrence, sentences such as "according to the story, there is some x such that x is Hamlet and x is a prince" can be true.

Although nonpostulating views of fictional discourse seem able to account for fictional discourse about fictional objects, that is, discourse about what happens in the story, they have far more trouble accounting for serious talk about fictional objects made from the real-world point of view. Not all discussions of works of literature involve describing the way things are represented in the story. Often, critical discourse requires that we step out of that context to speak from the real-world point of view about, for example, whether the characters and events represented are real or fictional, by whom and in what circumstances they were authored, what role they play in literary history, and so on. So the challenges of offering analyses of fictional discourse are not limited to analyzing sentences such as "Hamlet is a prince"; they must also be able to analyze sentences such as "Mr. Pickwick is a fictional character," "Emma Woodhouse was created by Jane Austen," and "Hamlet appears in *Hamlet* and *Rosencrantz and Guildenstern are Dead.*"

The usual technique of forcing sentences into the context of a prefix such as "according to the story" is of no help in these cases, for according to the relevant stories Pickwick is not a fictional character (but a real man), Emma Woodhouse was not created by Jane Austen (but by her parents), and Hamlet is not said to appear in any works of fiction. Thus troubles for nonpostulating views of fiction arise in trying to handle these sentences in ways that avoid referring to fictional characters but nonetheless correspond to our ordinary views about which sentences are true and which false. Even Ryle, one of the great originators and defenders of the paraphrase technique, offers blatantly inadequate readings of such sentences in "Systematically Misleading Expressions." If we want to use expressions like "Mr. Pickwick is a fiction," he suggests, all we can do is "say of Dickens 'there is a story-teller,' or of *Pickwick Papers* 'there is a pack of lies.' "[1] These clearly do not capture the meaning of the original sentence; they do not even distinguish Mr. Pickwick from any other character or distinguish lies from fiction.[2]

Those committed to the paraphrase technique have not gone without efforts to handle such sentences; on the contrary a great variety of solutions have been attempted.[3] Sentences such as "Mr. Pickwick is a fictional character" are often paraphrased by Russellians and Fregeans respectively as "[the name] 'Mr. Pickwick' does not denote" or "[the sense] *Mr. Pickwick*

95

does not present anything."[4] (Both of these would make equally true the [false] claim "Sblithers Scolby is a fictional character"). Claims about authorship might in like spirit be paraphrased as merely describing the actions of Jane Austen at a certain time and place – for example, that she wrote a story including the name "Emma Woodhouse." Claims about the appearance of a character in various literary works might be taken really to be about a sequence of words appearing in a text. Each of these paraphrases has its problems, problems that have been amply discussed elsewhere.[5] Moreover, as long as we only discuss the acts of authors and the appearance of words in texts it will be extremely difficult to set accurate conditions regarding whether we can with justice say that the same character, and not just the same name, appears in a work.

But these detailed failings have been well discussed; what I wish to point out is a deeper and more general problem that persists even if each individual paraphrase succeeds. To avoid the difficulties of fictional discourse, the paraphraser devises a great variety of ways of reconstruing sentences, all of which seem to be straightforward claims about fictional characters: In some cases we must take them to be, really, about names or senses; in other cases about the activities of real people; in others about sequences of words in texts, and so on. In short, for each case a different strategy is developed in an ad hoc manner merely to save the idea that we need not refer to fictional characters.

It is not that the paraphrase technique in general is a bad one. Certainly in discussing what happens in a story, paraphrasing sentences about what occurs within the context of a literary work as "according to the story" seems a natural and apt way of making the real form of the statement obvious. But the use of a paraphrase should be to reveal the genuine form of a sentence that might be obscured by its surface grammar, not to invent contorted restatements expressly to avoid reference to unwanted objects. The prospects for finding consistent and plausible paraphrases that avoid committing us to fictional objects seem slim at best, and the process hopelessly ad hoc. As Parsons comments, "The extent to which faith in the existence of an appropriate paraphrase outruns the believer's ability to give such a paraphrase is often quite striking."[6] Even if good paraphrases were available for all the cases commonly discussed (which seems not to be the case), we would have no assurance that an insurmountable case will not be discovered to render all of this patchwork pointless, or that these varied analyses will not come into conflict in analyzing complex sentences. In any case, a good theory is surely preferable to such ad hoc expedients, for a theory provides a systematic means of determining the truth-values of sentences of different kinds rather than working backwards from the apparent truth-value of different sentences to offer an a posteriori justification of why they get the truth-values commonly assigned to them.

There is an alternative analysis of language that likewise avoids postulating fictional objects and that has won many converts: Walton's pretense theory. Walton understands sentences occurring in the context of talking about the story as claims about what kinds of pretense are appropriately engaged in discussing the story. So, for example, if someone claims "Tom Sawyer attended his own funeral" this, on Walton's theory, is properly understood as the claim that:

The Adventures of Tom Sawyer is such that one who engages in pretense of kind K [claiming "Tom Sawyer attended his own funeral"] in a game authorized for it makes it fictional of himself in that game that he speaks truly.[7]

The fact that some kinds of pretense are more appropriate then others is, according to the pretense view, what gives these sentences the appearance of truth or falsity. (The pretense of expressing "Tom Sawyer was a humpbacked whale" is presumably inappropriate.)

When it comes to handling real predications of fictional objects, however, Walton's pretense theory does no better than its Fregean counterparts.[8] Pretense is certainly involved in some of our discourse about fictional characters and Walton is to be credited with revealing the central role of pretense in much of our experience of and discourse about fiction. It certainly seems, however, that we sometimes step *outside* the pretense, when we stop pretending that there are really such people and animals and instead talk of them straightforwardly as fictional characters that appear in stories, are created by authors, thought about by readers, and so on. Although the pretense view excels at explaining our talking *as if* there were a detective called "Holmes" and a prince called "Hamlet," without assuming there are such, it fails to take serious discourse about fictional characters seriously.

Walton uses the notion of "unofficial games" of make-believe to offer readings of various kinds of real predications about fictional objects that, he claims, do not threaten to force fictional objects on us. For example, he offers the following conjecture to explain the apparent truth of the statement "Gregor Samsa is a (purely fictional) character":

There may be an unofficial game in which one who says ["Gregor Samsa is a (purely fictional) character"] fictionally speaks the truth, a game in which it is fictional that there are two kinds of people: "Real" people and "fictional characters."[9]

Other seemingly serious statements such as "Sherlock Holmes is more famous than any other detective" he reads as:

There is a degree of fame such that no real detective is famous to that degree, and to pretend in a certain manner [in the manner in which one who says "Sherlock Holmes is famous to that degree" normally would be pretending] in a game authorized for the Sherlock Holmes stories is fictionally to speak truly (414).

Attributions of authorship such as "an author models a character on an existing character" are handled similarly as "it is fictional that he creates someone to be like some other person" (417).

Treating these as "more or less ad hoc unofficial" games of make-believe, without coded or conventional rules, some of which "no one has ever played or ever will," (425) first of all makes their usefulness in determining whether such statements are acceptable (fictionally true) or not extremely limited. Here we seem still farther from having a genuine and unified theory of fictional discourse that would allow us to determine the truth-values of sentences of different kinds. Instead, we have only a program for creating individualized apologetics that allow us to say after the fact that a certain sentence seems true because of its role in some ad hoc unofficial game.

Second and more important, it seems a case of implausibly forcing the data to fit the theory to count these as cases of nonliteral speech involved in a game of make-believe. The claim that Sherlock Holmes is famous (i.e., known about by many real people) seems on a par with claims that Marlon Brando is famous. Literary critics and other individuals making statements such as "Gregor Samsa is a fictional character" seem far from participating in a game of make-believe. On the contrary, the point of such remarks seems precisely to step outside of the game of make-believe, outside of the fictional world of the story, to say how things are from the real-world point of view, not to play some game in which authors are gods or parents. From the real-world point of view, Gregor Samsa, Sherlock Holmes, and the rest are not what the stories claim they are, but only fictional characters. If we were pretending that an author created a person, why use the term "character" to betray that pretense? Is it really more plausible to describe this as a case of invoking a new unauthorized game of make-believe and betraying it simultaneously, rather than describing it as the straightforward discourse it seems to be? The pretense theory seems to force us to construe all discourse about fictional characters as involving pretense. So doing forces us to radically, implausibly reinterpret much of the data present in our apparently straightforward talk about fictional objects.

It always seems bad policy in a philosophy of language to offer different analyses of sentences of the same type, occurring in the same sort of context, just on the basis of the types of object they are purportedly about. But paraphrase and pretense views alike, in their effort to avoid postulating fictional objects, run into this problem, for both such views must read external claims about fictional objects radically differently than similar sentences about real objects in order to avoid apparent reference to fictional characters. Although statements such as "*The Scarlet Letter* is a novel" and "the Old North Church was created in 1723" are read straightforwardly, paraphrase views require radical rewritings of similar sentences involving fictional objects such as "Hester Prynne is a fictional character" and "Sherlock Holmes was created in 1887." Similarly, although Walton would read the former pair of statements as straightforward assertions, the latter must be interpreted as cases wherein the speaker invents new games of pretense in which these assertions take part. But changing the analysis of a sentence not based on its syntax or context but merely based on the type of object purportedly referred to confuses issues of semantics and syntax and ill-advisedly mixes metaphysics into what should be a purely grammatical issue.

So those who do without fictional objects seem to encounter formidable difficulties in analyzing real predications about fictional objects. They also completely fail to offer a theory that would enable us to analyze such discourse in general, offering instead a series of piecemeal explanations for why each type of case acquires the truth-value that we are inclined to give it. The general attitude of the disbeliever in fiction is to hold tight to the view that we need not postulate fictional characters until someone brings forward a case of a sentence for which reference to a fictional character absolutely cannot be paraphrased away. As long as one permits ever new ad hoc paraphrases to be devised on all different models, such a counterexample may never be found.

That does not show, however, that disbelievers in fictional objects can rest easily. Quite the contrary, in evaluating other theories, such as scientific theories, the need to constantly adjust the theory with a series of ad hoc tinkerings to avoid apparent counterexamples would be taken as a sign of the theory's failure and need to be replaced. The issue is not whether one can devise some analysis of language that avoids reference to fictional objects, but what the best theory of language is, and whether it is one that accepts or denies that there are fictional objects referred to by fictional terms. It might be hoped that a smoother, more adequate, and less ad hoc analysis of language could be offered by admitting that there are fictional objects to which we can refer.

MEINONGIAN THEORIES

Those who postulate fictional objects typically take fictional discourse more at face value than their disbelieving peers, as they, for example, take sentences about fictional objects to be genuinely referring to objects. They then face the challenge of accounting for the apparent incoherences of fictional discourse without being brought into contradiction. This challenge has been met in two different ways: By distinguishing two kinds of property or by distinguishing two kinds of predication. Both techniques stem from the work of the Austrian philosopher (and student of Meinong) Mally.[10]

Parsons takes the first route in his Meinongian theory, distinguishing "nuclear" properties such as being tall, being blue, and being a detective from "extra nuclear" properties such as being possible, being complete, being fictional, and being thought about.[11] On Parsons' theory, predications of fictional objects such as "Hamlet is a prince" and "Sherlock Holmes is a detective" are handled straightforwardly, without the aid of a story operator. So Hamlet has the property of being a prince in just the same way that Charles Windsor does, and in general, fictional characters have all of those nuclear properties that the relevant story attributes to them (183).

One might suppose that treating inside predications as genuine predications (not inside the context of a story operator) would lead to contradiction: What about apparent contradictions such as Watson's war wound being in his arm and in his leg, or the round square being round and square? Admittedly, such cases do not present outright contradictions without the aid of additional principles, for example that a wound that is in the arm cannot be in the leg, or that an object that is round cannot be square. But according to Parsons's theory, although such principles might hold for existent objects, they simply do not hold true if we quantify over nonexistents as well. As Parsons writes, "If we read at one point that Watson's old war wound is in his leg, and we read elsewhere that it is in his arm, then Watson may turn out to be an impossible object" (184). The principles we normally assume about how having one property may exclude having another simply do not apply to the case of nonexistent objects.[12] Although this may make fictional objects impossible, in the sense that

100

no existing object could ever have these properties together, it does not prevent them from being objects, and it does not require that we give up the principle of noncontradiction.

As well as accepting that fictional objects may be impossible, Parsons accepts that fictional characters (and other nonexistents) may be incomplete objects that are indeterminate with respect to certain properties. According to the theory, the principle that for every property an object either has it or its (nuclear) negation holds good only for existent objects (19–20). So, for example, Hamlet may be just incomplete with respect to the property of having bloodtype A, for he neither has this property nor its (nuclear) negation (not having bloodtype A). Although all existing objects are complete, there is no reason to think that all nonexistent objects must be complete, too.

In short, Parsons's theory differs from the others in taking inside predications about fictional objects at face value and on a par with such predications about existing objects (so that Hamlet is a prince in the same sense as Charles is a prince, and the round square is round in the same way as a bicycle tire is round), and demonstrates that (and how) we can avoid inconsistency in constructing a Meinongian theory of nonexistent objects. His choice to handle predications about fictional objects as on a par with those about real objects does, however, bring about the prima facie disadvantage of forcing us to give up the idea that all objects are complete and to abandon general versions of ordinary principles about whether having one property excludes having another.

Zalta takes the other Mallian path in handling inside predications, distinguishing two modes of predication, which he calls "exemplifying" and "encoding."[13] Ordinary concrete objects exemplify their properties (exemplifying corresponds more or less to standard predication); abstract objects encode their nuclear properties.[14] Thus fictional characters encode exactly those properties that the story ascribes to them: Hamlet encodes being a prince, Sherlock Holmes encodes being a detective, and so on. An immediate consequence of this distinction is that on Zalta's theory, unlike Parsons's, Hamlet is not a prince in the same way in which Charles is, for whereas Charles exemplifies being a prince, Hamlet merely encodes being a prince. In this theory, ordinary principles regarding whether having one property excludes having another are maintained, as long as "having" is read as "exemplifying" and not "encoding." So, for example, nothing could exemplify being round and exemplify being square, although an object may encode being round and being square, and Watson's war wound may encode being in the arm and being in the leg. Similarly, even pairs of properties that seem outright contradictory can be encoded in the same object even though no object could exemplify them both: Although no object may exemplify the property of being round and not being round, an abstract object may encode the property of being round and not being round.[15] By the same token, objects must be complete with respect to the properties they exemplify (for every property P they must either exemplify P or not-P). But abstract objects may be incomplete with respect to the properties they encode: An object like Hamlet, who encodes just the properties ascribed to him in the play, can fail to encode being of bloodtype A and fail to encode not being of bloodtype A if neither of these attributes is ascribed to him in the story.

Thus each of these theories offers a means of handling fictional predications of fictional objects clearly and consistently. The main differences between them are, first, that Parsons's (unlike Zalta's) allows real and fictional individuals to have properties in just the same sense, so that the round square is round in the same sense as a bicycle tire is, and Hamlet is a prince in the same sense in which Charles is. Whether one counts this as an advantage or disadvantage depends on ones intuitions about how fictional characters have their properties. The other main difference is that Parsons gives up general principles about property exclusions for some kinds of object (nonexistent ones) and allows that there are incomplete objects, but Zalta allows only that objects may be incomplete with respect to the properties they encode and gives up principles about property exclusions for one mode of predication (encoding), allowing us to preserve these principles in the case of exemplification of properties.

Theories that do postulate fictional characters have a much easier time than nonpostulating theories in handling outside or real-world predications of fictional objects. On Parsons's theory, such sentences as "Holmes is a fictional character," "Holmes is admired by many real detectives," and (presumably) "Hamlet was created by Shakespeare" express true extranuclear predications of fictional objects.[16] On Zalta's theory, abstract objects such as fictional characters can exemplify certain extranuclear properties in addition to the properties they encode, so the above sentences, on his theory, are taken to describe properties that the abstract objects Holmes and Hamlet exemplify.[17] Thus far it seems that postulating fictional characters on a Meinongian model provides a relatively smooth and straightforward way of reading both internal and external statements about fictional characters.

Problems do not immediately fade, however, on postulating fictional objects. Meinongian theories require inelegant adjustments or ad hoc alterations in two areas: In developing the theories in ways that avoid apparent contradictions and in handling statements made about real objects in fictional contexts. In fact in the latter case, Meinongian theories have the same shortcoming as their pretense and paraphrase counterparts: Making ad hoc adjustments to their theories simply on the basis of the type of object referred to.

Dangers of falsehood or contradiction like those engendered by Meinong's famed existent golden mountain (which does not exist) may be circumvented by both Parsons's and Zalta's theories, but doing so involves complicating the initial simple picture with inelegant adjustments. On Parsons's theory, because existence is an extranuclear property, the golden mountain does not become endowed with existence simply by virtue of being ascribed it in what we might call the related "story"; indeed the existent golden mountain lacks the extranuclear property of existence. But Parsons, following up a suggestion of Meinong's, stipulates that every extranuclear property has associated with it a "watered-down" nuclear property, which *existent* objects have if and only if they have the extranuclear property. Thus the existent golden mountain differs from the (plain) golden mountain in that, in addition to the nuclear properties of being golden and being a mountain, it has the nuclear property of watered-down existence although it lacks the extranuclear property of existence.[18] Although this resolution avoids falsehood and contradiction and preserves the difference between the existent golden mountain and the (plain) golden mountain, introducing watered-down nuclear versions of extranuclear properties may seem unpleasantly ad hoc or mysterious.

Zalta's theory offers an alternative resolution to the same problem. According to his theory, the existent golden mountain is an abstract object that encodes goldenness, mountainhood, and existence; but it exemplifies nonexistence and so fails to exist (as an ordinary object). This resolution avoids the mystifying distinction between watered-down and full-strength properties, but it does complicate the theory by introducing a version of the two-kinds-of-property distinction in addition to the two-kinds-of-predication distinction, for abstract objects can only exemplify extranuclear properties. Allowing that abstract objects can exemplify certain properties introduces a certain amount of inelegance to the theory by disturbing the symmetry of having two kinds of objects, each of which lines up with its own mode of predication, and by introducing an odd feature that plays little role in the theory other than avoiding such difficulties (for example, the properties exemplified by abstract objects play no role in their identity conditions).

Greater difficulties arise for both Meinongian views in handling statements about real historical people and places that appear in literary works. Postulating views of fiction take fictional discourse such as "Hamlet is a prince" straightforwardly if it is about some fictional object, as describing some nuclear property had by Hamlet (Parsons) or some property encoded by Hamlet (Zalta). But suppose in some story Richard Nixon, instead of being elected president, marries a young queen, thereby becoming a prince. How are we to analyze the statement, also regarding a work of fiction and having the same form, "Nixon is a prince"? Parsons cannot read this in the same way as "Hamlet is a prince," for this would require maintaining that Nixon has the nuclear property of being a prince, which contradicts the documented empirical fact that he was never a prince. Similarly, Zalta cannot read this as describing a property encoded by Nixon, for it is a fundamental principle of the theory that ordinary objects (such as Nixon) cannot encode properties.[19]

Thus such views cannot read sentences in works of fiction about real individuals in the same way as parallel sentences about fictional characters – unless they take these sentences, too, to be about fictional characters. Parsons discusses this option, of having so-called surrogate fictional characters who appear in novels with the names (and many of the attributes) of real individuals. Unlike the real Nixon, a fictional surrogate Nixon could have the nuclear property of being a prince without contradicting empirical facts and (as an abstract object) could encode properties. But giving up the idea that real people and places (and not just their fictional surrogates) can appear in works of fiction would be giving up a great deal. Most works of historical fiction would lose much of their poignancy if they were not set amid real historical events and individuals, and fictionalized biographies or comedies often center on the idea that the lives of famous historical individuals went rather differently. Tom Stoppard's *Travesties*, for example, would lose much of its humor if it did not involve the real Lenin, Tristan Tzara, and James Joyce coming together in Vienna, but only some similar fictional individuals (in a similar fictional city). Parsons himself finds the idea of dealing exclusively in fictional surrogates unappealing and maintains that, although we may sometimes in special situations speak of fictional surrogate objects like "the London of the Holmes stories," it is the real objects themselves that appear in stories.[20]

If we are not content to say that a story can never be about a real person, place, or event, then the Meinongian has one other option available: Paraphrase. Thus, although the real Nixon was not a prince, he is such

104

that, according to the story, he was a prince; and although the real London is not such that it has a detective named "Holmes" residing in it, it is such that, according to the Doyle stories, it did. By such a method Meinongians can indeed allow that real individuals appear in works of fiction without contradicting known facts or theoretic principles. But there is a cost: Like the pretense and paraphrase views, it requires that we read sentences taken in the same context, with the same surface grammar, differently solely because they are about objects of a different type. The sentences "Hamlet is a prince" and "Nixon is a prince" might both appear in works of fiction, but although the former is read straightforwardly, the latter is read as shorthand for "according to the story, Nixon is a prince."

Such awkwardness in the most standard theories of fiction might indeed lead one to believe that – as far as analyses of language are concerned – there is no net gain to be achieved by postulating fictional objects. As we have seen them so far, both realist and antirealist theories of fictional discourse require ad hoc amendments to make them work; if the question is whether we can gain a better analysis of language with or without fictional characters at this stage it might seem like a draw. Perhaps it is for this reason that the real advantages to be gained by postulating fictional objects have yet to be recognized. But we should not so easily give up the search for a better analysis of fictional discourse.

THE ARTIFACTUAL THEORY

The problems surrounding fictional discourse may be resolved by recognizing that these problems stem from differences of contexts, not of objects. Two different contexts surround discussions concerning literary works and the events and creatures represented in them. One natural way of speaking is to speak within the fictional context, about what is true according to the story. It is clear that we are speaking within this context whenever we discuss what goes on and what characters are like in the story. Often some pretense is involved in such discussions, as we pretend that what the story says is true; for example, that it describes not mere fictional characters but instead actual people whom we could praise, criticize, or psychoanalyze. Such pretense renders the use of such phrases as "according to the story" unnecessary, as this is simply understood. I refer to these as "fictional contexts." But literary critical discourse does not always remain at the level of such fictional contexts. Often critical discourse involves speaking not from the internal perspective of what goes on in the story but from the external critic's perspective, speaking of these straightforwardly as fictional characters, created by authors in particular circumstances, providing paradigms of the 19th century Romantic heroine, and so on. I call these "real contexts."

In each context, we can talk about fictional objects or about real objects. Fictional contexts occur not only if we discuss what fictional characters are like according to the story, but also if real people, places, and events appear in works of fiction and we discuss them as they are portrayed in the story. Similarly, we can speak of fictional characters in real contexts, if we discuss their authorship or their place in literary history or assert that they are fictional characters, just as we can likewise (and most often do) speak of real people in real contexts, discussing them as historical individuals rather than as they are portrayed in any story. The homogeneous cases, concerning real predications of real objects and fictional predications of fictional objects, turn out to be relatively easy to handle for postulating and nonpostulating theories alike. This is perhaps not surprising, given that the predications we normally worry about the most are real ones in the case of real objects (dismissing the rest as mistakes or lies), and fictional ones in the case of fictional objects (as we discuss the traits of different characters and the events of their lives). But the opposite type of discourse does occur for each type of entity, and it is in these mixed cases that the real difficulties surface: Nonpostulating views seem to fail at handling real discourse about fictional objects, and even the postulating theories we have examined have to introduce a degree of inelegance to their theories to account for this. Fictional discourse about real objects, such as occurs if historical personages appear in works of fiction, presents even more serious difficulties for Meinongian views of fiction. We are left in need of a theory of fiction that can offer a smooth account of both kinds of predication of both kinds of object.

Once we separate the two contexts in which claims about literature may occur and allow that there are fictional characters to which we may refer, however, the resolution to the various difficulties surrounding fictional discourse is breathtakingly simple. Real predications, those made without pretense, outside of the context of what occurs in fictional works, may be taken straightforwardly as genuine predications attributing properties to entities, some of which are real and some of which are fictional. So sentences such as "Jimmy Carter is a person," "Notre Dame is a cathedral," and "Hamlet is a fictional character" should be treated in the same way, as genuine predications applied to the object referred to. Similarly, other statements from the real-world perspective, such as "Hamlet was created by Shakespeare," "Hamlet appears in more than one literary work," "Amy

Carter was created by her parents," and "Julius Caesar appears in more than one literary work" are to be evaluated straightforwardly, as unparaphrased discourse about objects that are, in some cases, fictional characters, in others, people.

On the other hand, whether they concern real or fictional objects, statements made in fictional contexts seem best understood as implicitly describing what is true according to the story. Statements such as "Hamlet is a prince" and "Nietzsche was psychoanalyzed by Freud"[21] occur in the contexts of literary works and are not literally true although they describe states of affairs that, according to the relevant stories, do obtain regarding the fictional character Hamlet and the real people Nietzsche and Freud. Even if story operators have been a congenial solution for those who wish to avoid fictional objects, that does not mean that anyone who reads fictional predications as implicitly within the context of such an operator is committed to an antirealist view. Although I take some straightforward statements about fictional characters to be true and argue that we should claim that fictional objects exist, I nonetheless contend that the appropriate reading of fictional predications is in the context of a prefix such as "according to the story." "Hamlet is a prince," for example, should be taken as shorthand for "according to the (relevant) play, Hamlet is a prince." What is true according to the story is, roughly, a combination of what is explicitly said in the story and what is suggested by the background knowledge and assumptions on which the story relies. Put in other terms, it is what a competent reader would understand to be true according to the story.[22] Much has been written that is sensible on the topic of how, more precisely, to understand what is true according to the story, so I shall not unnecessarily add to the literature here.[23]

Understanding statements in fictional contexts as implicitly prefixed with "according to the story" avoids many difficulties. First, we need not accept that fictional characters may be impossible or incomplete objects (which ought to make them much more palatable than traditional Meinongian nonexistents). For the round square is not both round and square, it is such that, according to Meinong's story it is round, and according to Meinong's story it is square. Nor is Hamlet incomplete by being neither of bloodtype A nor not of bloodtype A. Because these claims seem to treat Hamlet as a human being who has blood, it seems most likely that such statements would be made in a fictional context, in which case they should be read as "according to *Hamlet*, Hamlet is of bloodtype A" and "according to *Hamlet*, it is not the case that Hamlet is of bloodtype A." Both of these are false, because the story does not mention anything about it. But because these sentences do not describe real properties of Hamlet, but only how he is said to be according to the story, we need not infer on that basis that Hamlet is incomplete with respect to the property *being of bloodtype A*.[24]

Another advantage of this method of handling fictional discourse is that we can provide a sense in which fictional statements about real individuals are true without asserting falsehoods about historical figures or shifting to surrogate fictional counterparts. For although the simple sentence "Nietzsche was psychoanalyzed by Freud" is not true, the expanded statement "according to *When Nietzsche Wept* Nietzsche was psychoanalyzed by Freud" is true. The procedure applies in the same way to fictional characters that immigrate to other stories. We do not need to separate the Guildenstern of *Hamlet* from the Guildenstern of *Rosencrantz and Guildenstern Are Dead*, treating them as two separate characters, to avoid the problems of differing or contradictory properties that may be assigned the character in different works. If Guildenstern loses 89 gold pieces in *Rosencrantz and Guildenstern Are Dead* but not in *Hamlet*, this is merely a surface inconsistency. For these sentences can be read as (one and the same Guildenstern is such that) according to *Rosencrantz and Guildenstern Are Dead* he loses 89 gold pieces, but it is not the case that according to *Hamlet* he loses 89 gold pieces. On this reading, one and the same Guildenstern can be ascribed both properties without difficulty, and so we need not conclude that there are two different Guildensterns (or one impossible Guildenstern).

One area of particular difficulty in analyzing fictional discourse concerns modal discourse about fiction. On the one hand we require a way to account for the apparent truth of claims such as "Holmes might have never been created" and "Meursault (of *The Stranger*) might not have killed the Arab," and on the other hand we need a way to analyze certain claims that might leave us simply confused: Is Sherlock Holmes essentially clever? Might Brick of *Cat on a Hot Tin Roof* become an abusive father?

The apparent difficulties that surround modal discourse about fiction also quickly dissolve if we make use of this general method of handling fictional discourse. The same distinction between claims in fictional contexts (to be read in the context of a story prefix) and claims in real contexts (to be read straightforwardly) may be made with respect to modal discourse about fiction. Thus we should distinguish real-context claims such as "if Arthur Conan Doyle's medical career had been more successful, Sherlock Holmes might have never been created," from fictional-context claims

108

such as "although Watson had six cuts on the inside of his left shoe, he could have had merely five," and "Meursault could have refrained from killing the Arab."

The status of fictional characters as dependent entities makes certain real-context modal truths about them immediately apparent. Fictional characters are essentially created entities, so it is true, for example, that Sherlock Holmes is necessarily created. Any world in which a character appears is a world in which it is created, and indeed each fictional character is necessarily such that it was created by those particular creative acts that in fact created it. Contingent external truths about fictional characters include such statements as: It is possible that Sherlock Holmes would have never been created if Doyle's medical career had gone better, and it is possible that Holmes would have remained unknown were it not for the interest of *Lippincott's Magazine*; Dmitri Karamazov might have never been created had it not been for the stability given Dostoyevsky's life through his marriage to Anna Snitkina.

But many of those modal statements we care most about regarding fictional characters are not external statements like those above but statements in fictional contexts describing how the characters' lives might have varied from those set out in the work of literature. Analyzing such fictional-context statements is somewhat trickier than analyzing the corresponding real-context statements, and indeed at first we may not know what to say about some claims of this variety.

The trickiness of analyzing these claims stems from the fact that, in their simple forms, these statements are ambiguous. For if (as I have suggested) we read fictional-context statements as implicitly in the context of a story operator, there are at least three plausible readings of such sentences, according to how we read the scope of the modal operator and that of the story operator. Thus, for example, "Meursault could have refrained from killing the Arab" could be read as:

A. There is some story (*The Stranger*) such that according to it, it is possible that Meursault refrained from killing the Arab.

or as:

B. There is some story (*The Stranger*) such that, it is possible that, according to it, Meursault refrained from killing the Arab.

or as:

C. Possibly, there is some story such that, according to it, Meursault refrained from killing the Arab.

I think statements of type A – that there is some story such that, according to it, it is possible that . . . – are what we usually mean when we inquire after such internal modal statements about fictional characters. In this case, A is surely true under any reasonable interpretation of the novel, indeed it is one of the keys to the novel. But it does not describe killing the Arab as a contingent property of the character, for the ascription is within the scope of the story operator. Similarly, on an A-style reading, "It is possible that Watson has other than six cuts on his shoe," is true, for according to the story, the cuts were caused by a careless servant, and certainly the Holmes stories incorporate enough of our ordinary background assumptions to ensure that according to the story, it remains possible that one not hire a certain servant, or that the servant be careless in a slightly different way. In any case, once the alternatives are laid out, it seems fairly clear that readings such as A are what we mostly have in mind. This provides us with a reasonable way of reading and inquiring after the truth-value of such internal modal statements and accounting for the sense in which statements such as those above are true. But we can do so without having to broach the question of whether being clever is an essential property of Holmes or being a murderer is an essential property of Meursault. For these are, on this theory, not properties of the characters at all, but only properties they are ascribed in the relevant stories.

Analyzing claims such as B – that there is some story, such that it is possible that, according to it . . . – brings us into deeper issues regarding the identity conditions of stories. It seems that claims such as B are seldom if ever what we mean by our internal modal claims about fiction and probably would arise only in a philosophical discussion about story identity; thus I do not pursue these here.[25]

But even if A provides an appropriate reading of many modal claims about fiction, often we make modal claims – about what might happen to a character after the story is over, or what would have happened if a pivotal event had turned out differently – regarding which the actual story has nothing to say or imply one way or the other. Thus if we wish for any of these to come out as true we need a different means of reading these sentences. Such claims might be read on the model of C: Possibly there is *some* story, such that, according to it . . . . If we claim that Brick of *Cat on a Hot Tin Roof* could become an abusive father, or could have been a successful football player, we might mean that possibly, there is some story (perhaps a sequel) in which Brick has a child but fails to overcome his alcoholism and tendency to violence, or, on the other hand, that a different story could be written in which Brick had not fallen into depression and had become a successful athlete, but in which he is recognizably and

110

believably the same character. Such alternate stories are sometimes even composed to make claims like these particularly compelling; often it is when we have such alternate stories in mind that we make such claims. Whether one counts C as true depends on whether one is willing to allow that the same character can appear in more than one story, and under what conditions. Because the artifactual theory allows this (on the condition the author of the second work is competently acquainted with the character as in the first story and intends to import that character into her or his work), it has the advantage of enabling some such claims to come out as true.

In short it seems that we may mean many different things if we make modal claims about fictional characters. By treating fictional characters as dependent abstracta we can offer straightforward and sensible readings of external modal claims about fictional characters such as those that they might have never been created or never been discovered. Moreover, distinguishing fictional and real contexts and reading claims in fictional contexts as implicitly prefixed with "according to the story" enables us to unravel a variety of ambiguities in fictional-context modal claims about fictional characters, dispel our confusions in facing internal modal claims, and provide readings appropriate to the context.

This method of analyzing predications about fictional objects should alleviate worries that postulating fictional objects will get one into trouble and so remove one more stumbling block to admitting fictional objects to our ontology. More importantly, the ability to offer parallel analyses for fictional objects and real objects in the cases of both real discourse and fictional discourse should reduce the impression that fictional objects present a special case, wherein unique difficulties arise for a theory of language. The same sorts of problems arise in each case, and the same sorts of solutions are available for fictional and real objects alike.

OBJECTIONS AND ASSESSMENT

Fictional discourse is, admittedly, an area in which there are confusions and apparent inconsistencies that need to be sorted out. Doing so involves certain costs in terms of reinterpreting some of the apparent claims we make about fictional characters, so there are invariably certain trade-offs involved in producing a consistent and workable analysis of fictional discourse. Here, the analyses offered by the artifactual theory are no different. The trade-offs arise in that two types of claims we naturally make regarding fictional characters – that they do not exist, and that they have certain of the properties attributed to them in literary works – both turn out to

111

be literally false in this theory. One has to paraphrase somewhere to avoid contradictions or falsehoods; my own view is that there are very natural paraphrases of both of these types of claim according to which they are true, paraphrases that I think do reveal what we really mean in making such shorthand claims. That should soften the blow of having to give up the idea that such statements are literally true and make these inevitable costs more palatable.

The first part of the objection focuses on the fact that, in this theory, whether we analyze them as real or as fictional predications, claims to the effect that Sherlock Holmes and Hamlet exist come out as true. For the characters Holmes and Hamlet really exist, and according to the relevant stories Holmes and Hamlet really exist as well (although according to the stories they are people, not fictional characters). But, it might be objected, there is some perfectly good sense in which claims such as "Sherlock Holmes *does not* exist" are true. Walton casts the challenge to views that postulate fictional objects as follows: "Believers must confront the fact that, in many contexts, we easily and naturally deny that there is a Lear and that there are such things as dragons and unicorns."[26]

The intuition that there is no Lear nor any unicorns, and the fact that we quite naturally deny their existence, are easily accommodated without denying that there are such *fictional characters.* Statements like "there is no Lear" or "there are no unicorns" are quite naturally interpretable as claims that, despite what the stories say, "there is no (real) person who is Lear" or "there are no (real) animals that are unicorns." Indeed, such denials are often phrased in such terms as "there's no such person (he's only fictional)" or "there are no such animals (they are mythical figures)." These statements, naturally, remain true in the present theory, as in any sensible theory of fictional objects. So nonexistence claims regarding fictional characters in general are true provided that they are understood as shorthand for claims to the effect that there is no such (real) man, no such (real) animal, and so on. Implicitly limiting the sorts of entities one is quantifying over is in fact something we do all the time in our discourse, when our audience normally understands us to only be referring to relevant items. As Parsons points out, we do so quite readily if we speak of cows or crockery, meaning to refer only to those items we own:

In ordinary linguistic interchanges a limited range of things are under discussion, and both speaker and hearer take the common nouns that they use to be implicitly restricted to these things. Without such an assumption communication would be extremely difficult, if not impossible.[27]

112

Precisely such an implicit limitation is what is meant if we make nonexistence claims about fictional characters, which should not be surprising given the fact that the presence of fictional detectives and fictional beasts is of little relevance to practical matters of life like solving crimes and being transported. The suitability of this understanding of claims that Holmes and the rest do not exist is reinforced by noting intuitions on the other side: If asked whether such *fictional characters* as Holmes or Hamlet exist, those uncorrupted by philosophy invariably say "yes," puzzled by why someone would ask such a silly question.

The second objection centers on the fact that the analyses offered make claims such as "Hamlet is a prince" or "Holmes is a detective" literally false (although if paraphrased with "according to the story" they are, of course, true). But even the average person explaining the sense in which such claims are true, to someone who does not understand the implicit fictional context, may appeal to their paraphrased form. If pressed by some uncomprehending child, we would admit that Hamlet is really only a fictional character, and so one cannot meet him as one can a real prince (although the story describes him as being a real person whom one could meet); and Nietzsche was not really psychoanalyzed by Freud (the story just says he was). I think that we should take seriously the fact that we make reference to the story if we explain the sense in which such claims are true, for this suggests that statements such as that Holmes is a detective really are shorthand for a longer locution such as "according to the story, Holmes is a detective." Thus it seems to me that, because some trade-offs are demanded, these are not bad ones to make, because we can so easily explain the sense in which these claims are true, and in ways that make sense of our ordinary ways of considering fictional characters.

On the other hand, these analyses bring with them many counterbalancing advantages that should make evident the advantages of postulating fictional characters for developing a good theory of language. They should alleviate some common worries that remain with traditional Meinongian views of fiction by offering a view that does not require postulating strange objects that may be incomplete or combining properties impossible for normal objects to combine. Finally, they are able to overcome the problems Meinongian views encounter in handling fictional discourse about real individuals and to handle fictional discourse about real and fictional individuals on a par.

Most importantly, postulating fictional characters as abstract artifacts and analyzing discourse about fictional and real objects in the same way enables us to offer a better theory of language than those views that attempt to avoid fictional objects at all costs. Allowing that some real, unprefixed predications can be made regarding fictional objects but maintaining a uniform reading of real predications as straightforward, and of predications in fictional contexts as implicitly prefixed with a story operator, yields a theory that enables us to preserve the intuitive classifications of whether sentences of each type are true or false and determines the truth-values for such statements in general rather than offering a piecemeal a posteriori analysis of such sentences. Finally, unlike rivals of both types, this theory analyzes statements about real objects and fictional objects in the same way rather than ill-advisedly shifting the way we read a sentence merely on the basis of the type of object it concerns. Even if we might be able to offer a theory of language without fictional characters, we can do much better with them.

114

8

Ontology and Categorization

I have argued that we can offer better analyses of experience and language by postulating fictional characters, but before deciding to admit them these benefits must be weighed against the ontological costs. It is generally supposed that these costs are high, for admitting fictional characters, it is thought, involves postulating a new category of extremely strange and unusual entities, thus taking on a large burden compared with the parsimony which could be maintained without them. These worries should be taken seriously but should not be left unexamined. Does admitting fictional characters require positing a strange new category of beings bloating an otherwise spare ontology? Do the costs in terms of parsimony outweigh the benefits gained in analyzing experience and discourse? To properly assess the ontological costs of admitting fictional characters we must step back to ask how we can make such ontological decisions in a principled and consistent manner rather than on the basis of vague fears or aesthetic preferences for what seems to be a sparser ontological landscape.

PIECEMEAL ONTOLOGY VERSUS CATEGORIAL ONTOLOGY

Ontology is a two-part venture. The first task is to lay out categories in which things might be claimed to exist, without commitment to whether or not such categories are occupied. The second task is that of assessing what there really is.[1] Contemporary ontologists typically – although not always – focus exclusively on the second task and proceed on a one-by-one basis to argue for or against allowing certain kinds of things, be they numbers, universals, acts of consciousness, or fictional objects, into our ontology.

This ontological method I call the "piecemeal approach," for it involves giving separate hearing to arguments for and against postulating each type of entity and deciding piecemeal what to admit in each case based on the strengths of the available arguments and guided by the principle of parsimony. But taken on its own, a piecemeal approach cannot provide the basis for a comprehensive and systematic ontology. For what is at issue in developing an ontology is what kinds of entities one admits. Suppose one took a pure piecemeal approach to ontology, attempting to determine what entities to postulate without making use of a system of relevant categories. In the absence of a system of categories, one would be forced to address separately any purported "kind" of entity grouped together in an everyday classification, be it cookware, woodwinds, sporting goods, or baseball games. There are far too many such sorts of entities to address in a one-at-a-time manner; because entities may be grouped together in an infinite number of ways, proceeding in a genuinely piecemeal fashion cannot yield a comprehensive or systematic view of what there is.

Moreover, taking such a piecemeal approach to ontology by addressing separately whether or not we should accept various sorts of entity is not only prohibitively time-consuming but dangerous, for it has inherent risks of inconsistency or arbitrariness. If each purported type of entity is treated separately without considering beforehand what the relevant similarities and differences among kinds are, the piecemeal ontologist runs the risk of arbitrarily rejecting some entities but accepting others that are relevantly similar, or even of accepting one sort of entity but rejecting entities on which they depend, and thus offering an inconsistent ontology. Thus a pure piecemeal approach to ontology can only provide a patchy view of what there is and a view that always risks arbitrariness and inconsistency.

In practice it seems that no one really approaches ontology in a purely piecemeal manner, evaluating the claims of arbitrarily selected groups of purported entities. Instead, decisions to consider some groups (such as abstracta, numbers, or fictional characters) rather than others are motivated by background beliefs about which groupings are ontologically relevant categories. But if background ideas about which categories are relevant are to be invoked, surely it is better to discuss and present such categories up front, so that they can be evaluated and revised, rather than working from shadowy intuitions about which groups seem relevant.

Even the primary tool of piecemeal ontology, Ockham's razor, presupposes a categorization into relevant types. For what is at issue in ontological parsimony is not how many entities in number, but what basic kinds of entities one accepts. An ontology is not more parsimonious if it rejects one group of entities but accepts another group that is relevantly similar. One cannot, for example, offer a more parsimonious ontology by rejecting the characters of mystery stories but accepting those of spy novels; so doing would be a case of false parsimony. Thus we cannot evaluate the relative parsimony of different ontologies, or determine whether eliminating certain groups of entities makes a theory more parsimonious, without utilizing a system of relevant ontological categories.

To make a comprehensive and systematic appraisal of what there is, we need to supplement the need criterion with a prior system of categories drawn out according to criteria relevant for making ontological decisions and outlining what sorts of things there *might be* without prejudging the issue of what there is. A system of categories should meet two minimal criteria of adequacy. First, it must be exhaustive. If a categorial ontology is to be used as the basis for making ontological decisions without prejudging the issue of what there is, then it must have a place for everything there might be – in a strong sense, for everything thinkable – to ensure that nothing is left out. Secondly, to be genuine categories they must be mutually exclusive, so that everything falls under *exactly one* category.[2]

Because standard ways of doing ontology tacitly presuppose a system of categories, returning to a two-step approach to ontology provides a way of being open about what category system is presupposed and of making sure that it satisfies minimal criteria such as these. Against the backdrop of a categorial system we can make ontological decisions wholesale by deciding which of these categories are occupied and which are empty. Approaching ontological decisions globally avoids the dangers of inconsistency and false parsimony that may result from piecemeal ontology.

Furthermore, it provides a better means of making particular decisions about whether to admit controversial entities such as mathematical objects, universals, or fictional characters into our ontology, for we can begin by asking the simpler question of where such entities would fit on our system of categories. We can then evaluate the potential costs and benefits of eliminating these entities by examining whether eliminating them would (given our other ontological commitments) provide genuine or only false parsimony.

TRADITIONAL CATEGORIES AND SOURCES OF SKEPTICISM

Yet despite their potential usefulness, systems of categories have largely fallen out of favor and out of use. Although there have been a few notable exceptions in recent years, including new category systems proposed by Chisholm, Hoffman and Rosenkrantz, Johansson, and Grossmann, category systems are seldom used in making ontological decisions about whether to admit or reject entities of a certain type.[3] Category systems have been sidelined in contemporary ontology in part owing to general and pervasive skepticism about categorization. In some cases this takes the form of an explicit categorial relativism. Collingwood and Körner, for example, explicitly embrace a relativism about category schemes, treating them not as categorizations of what there is or might be, but rather as mere reflections of the varying metaphysical presuppositions of an individual or age.[4] Perhaps more commonly, the skepticism takes the form of a tacit disbelief that traditional category systems really offer a mutually exclusive and exhaustive list, leading ontologists to eschew the idea of categorization altogether and proceed on a piecemeal basis to assess whether to posit entities of a given type. I suggest that, although this skepticism is not baseless, the sources of skepticism may be to a great extent overcome by working from a multidimensional system of categories.

Traditional systems of categories postulate a single dimension of categories either in parallel or in a tree-type hierarchy. Aristotle's categories (substance, quantity, quality, relation, place, date, posture, state, action, and passion) form an example of a parallel system of ten highest categories without a single higher category to subsume them; Johansson's nine highest categories (space-time, state of affairs, quality, external relation, grounded relation, inertia, spontaneity, tendency, and intentionality) are similarly laid out as parallel highest kinds.

Others such as Chisholm and Rosenkrantz and Hoffman arrange their categories in porphyrian trees.[5] A tree-type categorial system, as Hoffman and Rosenkrantz describe it, "is a hierarchical system of genera and species in which every ontological category is a genus or species."[6] Thus, to be a well-formed categorial system in this model likewise requires staying within a single dimension of categorization, laying out only more specific kinds under the more general kinds at each higher level.

Problems leading to skepticism arise both within and among such one-dimensional category systems. The first form of skepticism stems from a lack of conviction, in looking at a single system of categories, that this set of categories really provides an exhaustive and mutually exclusive set of categories. If we are presented with a simple list such as Aristotle's, or a tree such as Chisholm's, it is difficult to know how we can be certain that the system meets the criteria of exhaustiveness and mutual exclusivity. Aristotle's scheme, for example, risks violating mutual exclusivity:

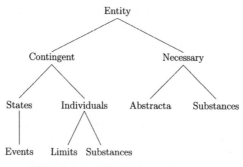

FIGURE 8.1   Chisholm's category system.

States seem to be a kind of relation, so being armed would fall into both of these categories.[7]

Whether in parallel or hierarchical form, a one-dimensional scheme is simply unable to capture all relevant distinctions. In some cases cross-over categories seem inevitable, but they are not expressible in a simple parallel or hierarchical scheme. This problem becomes visible in Chisholm's category system (Fig. 8.1), which risks violating both the constraints of the one-dimensional tree structure and the exhaustiveness criterion. His system of categories is based on a primary division into the contingent and the necessary, each of which is further divided into categories.

Categories such as substance and event seem orthogonal to those of the contingent and the necessary; no doubt this is why substance unhappily appears as the terminus of two different branches of the tree, allowing for both contingent and necessary substances (a problem that Hoffman and Rosenkrantz point to as violating the form of the tree structure).[8] Although some cross-overs of orthogonal distinctions creep into this one-dimensional system, however, they are not made systematically. As a result, it seems that the system is not exhaustive, for it arbitrarily omits such possibilities as those of necessary events and contingent abstracta, the latter of which, as I argue in Chapter 3, is a live option that seems particularly well suited for classifying such entities as universals, the constructivist's mathematical entities, and literary works.

The second source of skepticism comes not from within any single system of categories but from the diversity of category systems devised from Aristotle to the present day. For example, a system of categories such as Aristotle's seems so irreconcilably different from Descartes's two main categories of the mental and the material that they appear arbitrary and unrelated, leading to the view that category systems are no reflection of reality but only of the individual presuppositions of the philosopher drawing them out or of the age in which they are believed.

Rather than retreat to relativism, I offer a different analysis. Any system of categories is an abstraction from things in all of their particularity to the highest genera under which they fall. Categorizations thus inevitably leave out some of the peculiarities of the objects under discussion. The embarrassing diversity of category systems laid out by philosophers from Aristotle onward bears witness to the fact that this abstracting may be done in different ways, based on different aspects of a thing. The resulting categorial systems are often mutually orthogonal, but they lie in a wider multidimensional space of possibilities. Rather than abandoning attempts at categorization, we should seek a broader, multidimensional category system able to track and systematize these variations.

In the remainder of this chapter I draw out the beginnings of such a system. I attempt to show how, from a unified basis, one can draw out a single category system within which such diverse traditional categories as the concrete and the abstract, the real and the ideal, and the material and the mental can be located. Unlike traditional parallel or tree-type systems, this system of categorization is multidimensional, enabling various mutually orthogonal systems of categories to be incorporated. For present purposes I limit myself to drawing out a category system based on two separate axes, although in principle the scheme could be extended. I make no claim that this is the single correct final and fully adequate category system; I do claim, however, that it is exhaustive, is more comprehensive than traditional schemes, and isolates a number of features relevant to ontological decision making.

SYSTEM OF EXISTENTIAL CATEGORIES

Often the abstraction from a diversity of objects to a system of categories is explicitly or tacitly based on the syntactic categories of the words referring to those entities; this seems to lie behind common divisions into formal categories such as object, property, and state of affairs (corresponding to nominative, predicative, and propositional expressions). I draw out instead a system of categories based on the existence conditions of the things themselves. It might thus be labeled an "existential" rather than a "formal" categorization, and remains orthogonal to such formal categorizations.[9]

In particular, I focus on whether or not, and in what way, a thing materially depends on spatiotemporal entities and mental states for its existence.[10] Thus the categories delineated presuppose three primitive concepts: The relation of dependence, as discussed in Chapter 2; the property *being real*, in the sense of having a spatiotemporal location[11]; and the property *being a mental state*. Those mental states at issue here are primarily those exhibiting intentionality, for it is this intrinsic ability of certain mental states to represent something beyond themselves that seems able to support new properties and objects on top of the independent natural world. Nonetheless, because there may be some simple mental states lacking intentionality, I speak more generally of mental states.

Three objections might be raised to drawing out a system of categories in this way. First, it might seem odd to draw out categories based on a thing's dependence relations; because relational properties are commonly thought to have little to do with a thing's essence, categorizing things on the basis of certain relations they exhibit might seem perverse. But what we are really categorizing things with respect to is not some external relation such as what they are taller than or to the left of (that would indeed be perverse); instead it is with regard to the conditions for the existence of the object itself. A thing's existence conditions are absolutely central to characterizing it and drawing out its identity conditions and are centrally relevant to determining whether or not to postulate it, for they demonstrate what other sorts of entities must also be postulated, because its existence presupposes theirs.

Others might object that choosing dependencies on spatiotemporal entities and mental states as the dependencies to focus on is arbitrary. As should become clear in this chapter, choosing dependencies on real entities and mental states is far from arbitrary, for it captures the crux of ontological distinctions such as that between the abstract and the concrete, the material and the mental, the real and the ideal; and of controversies regarding whether to admit such entities as mathematical objects, fictional characters, mental states, social objects, and universals. The scheme could be extended to more dimensions to accommodate other concerns, but the centrality of these issues as poles of debate makes dependencies on the mental and the real an obvious place to begin in drawing out a multi-dimensional system of categories.

Finally, some might find it inappropriate to begin from real entities or mental states as a basis, because certain idealists or eliminative materialists would deny the existence of such entities. Rejecting this scheme because some deny the existence of real entities or mental states would be to misunderstand the nature of a categorial ontology. For these categories are to be drawn out in a prepartisan way, before making decisions about what should and should not be admitted. This procedure is particularly important for the would-be eliminativist or idealist. Even the eliminativist or idealist must acknowledge that these purported entities play a central role in the common-sense, apparent ontology that they seek to revise. Making clear what seems to depend on the mental or on spatiotemporal entities also makes clear what the apparent costs are of eliminating the supporting entities and so demonstrates where the eliminativist or idealist will have to do without entities or offer an alternative account of them.

Using dependence relations as the basis for drawing out categories brings several additional advantages. Dependence is itself sometimes used as a criterion for rejecting purported entities; indeed many reductionist programs consider *anything* dependent to be "nothing ontologically extra."[12] Perhaps more importantly, the dependencies among entities of different types place strong consistency constraints on an ontology, for one could not consistently accept entities of type A but reject those of type B, if type A entities depend on those of type B. Using dependence relations to mark out our categories provides a means of making these consistency constraints visible, and of maintaining the central role of a purported entity's dependencies in determining whether or not it should be postulated.

Drawing out a system of categories in terms of the ways in which an entity does or does not (ultimately) depend on spatiotemporal entities and mental states yields a set of categories that, unlike other systems, guarantees exhaustiveness and mutual exclusivity, thereby eliminating the first source of skepticism. Because the categories are drawn out in terms of the ways entities do or do not depend on mental states and real entities, the law of the excluded middle ensures that every entity is located somewhere in the categories that result, making the categories jointly exhaustive. Separating off mere dependence from historical dependence (and so forth) ensures that the categories are mutually exclusive.

Some of the most interesting varieties of dependence have been discussed in Chapter 2. Here we can make use of material relations of dependence, constant dependence, and historical dependence in both rigid and generic versions to draw out a system of ontological categories. The relations among types of dependence discussed at the close of Chapter 2 have important consequences for what categories are possible and what ontological systems are consistent:

1. Constant dependence entails historical dependence.
2. Historical dependence entails dependence.

In addition, if we assume that anything that is a mental state is necessarily a mental state, and that anything real is necessarily real, we can add the following:

3. If α is rigidly dependent/historically dependent/constantly dependent on β, and β is real, then α is generically dependent/historically dependent/constantly dependent on there being something real.
4. If α is rigidly dependent/historically dependent/constantly dependent on β, and β is a mental state, then α is generically dependent/historically dependent/constantly dependent on there being something that is a mental state.

The entailment relations among different kinds of dependence are represented schematically in Figure 8.2.

Figure 8.3 depicts the resultant category system. It consists of two separate (but structurally parallel) charts of categories drawn out on the basis of the definitions of dependence and the relations among them. These should be considered two aspects in a single system of classification, an entity's place in the scheme being determined by both its dependencies on mental states and its dependencies on spatiotemporal entities. Because there are ten boxes on each chart, there are 100 categories formed of their possible combinations. The two aspects of classification could be lined up on different axes, resulting in a unified diagram on which we could locate each type of entity in a single category. Because each subdiagram has two axes, the resultant unified diagram would be four-dimensional; the difficulty of drawing a four-dimensional diagram is the motive for leaving the charts separate. Nonetheless, these should be thought of not as separate

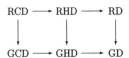

FIGURE 8.2. Entailment relations among kinds of dependence, using "RCD" to abbreviate "rigidly constantly dependent," "RHD" for "rigidly historically dependent," "RD" for "rigidly dependent," "GCD" for "generically constantly dependent," "GHD" for "generically historically dependent," and "GD" for "generically dependent."

Dependence on Real Entities   Dependence on Mental States

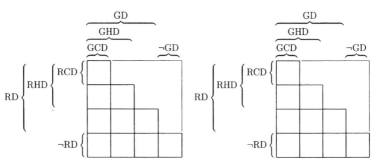

FIGURE 8.3   Ontological categories.

systems of categories but as two aspects of classification contributing to a single category system. The categories into which different entities fall may be by compared by means of the footprints that mark its location in each of the two charts.

The labels of each chart should be read down the rows and columns indicated by the brackets; so, for example, everything in the first column is generically constantly dependent, everything in the first two columns is generically historically dependent, and so on. The inclusion of the constant dependence column within the historical dependence columns and of the historical dependence columns within the dependence columns (and likewise for rows) reflects the implications among different kinds of dependence noted previously, ensuring that everything that is constantly dependent is historically dependent, but allowing that something may be historically dependent and yet not constantly dependent. The bottom row represents those entities that are not rigidly dependent, and the far right column represents entities not generically dependent (and so not dependent at all). Note that on each chart six categories are eliminated: Because nothing can be rigidly constantly dependent without being generically constantly dependent, there can be nothing that is rigidly constantly dependent and merely generically historically dependent or generically dependent, nor can there be something that is rigidly historically dependent and merely generically dependent, nor, finally, can there be something that is rigidly dependent and yet not generically dependent.

FAMILIAR CATEGORIES

A variety of familiar categories such as the material and the mental, the real and the ideal, and the abstract and the concrete may all be located in

Dependence on Mental States

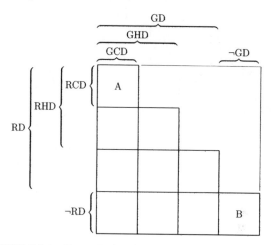

FIGURE 8.4 Categories based in dependence on mental states.

this multidimensional classification system. The two axes of classification based on dependence on the mental and dependence on the real correspond to the different dimensions of classification drawn out by category systems based in bifurcations respectively into the mental and the material, and the abstract and the concrete. Descartes's major division into the material and the mental, still tacitly used as a categorial system even by those who would deny the existence of anything in the category of the mental, may be recast in terms of the divisions in Figure 8.4. Mental states themselves (in virtue of their rigid constant dependence on themselves) belong in the upper-left box of Figure 8.4 (box A); purely material entities (on a realist view) belong in the lower right box (box B). Once we draw it out in these terms and in the context of an exhaustive system of categories it becomes clear that there is a great variety of categories in between the mental and the purely material, categories suitable for things that, although not mental states themselves, exhibit dependencies on the beliefs or practices of an individual or community.

The division between the real and the ideal may be located on the other axis based in dependencies on spatiotemporal entities. Ideal entities are characterized as existing independently of all real entities: An ideal entity can exist even if there is nothing that is real. This, of course, is the category to which numbers as well as Platonic universals are normally assigned (Fig. 8.5, box D). But if real entities are to be understood as those individuals with a definite spatiotemporal location (Fig. 8.5, box A),

Dependence on Real Entities

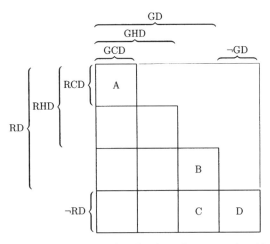

FIGURE 8.5   Categories based in dependence on real entities.

then clearly the real and the ideal are contraries at opposite ends of the spectrum and there are far more kinds of nonspatiotemporally located things than just ideal entities. These include types of things that, despite the fact that they are not located in space–time, do depend on real entities, as well as kinds of things that lack a spatiotemporal location but have a temporal origin. This, of course, is the space required to accommodate abstract artifacts from literary works to laws to models of car.

The issue of where the standard division between the abstract and the concrete falls on these categories is complicated in a way that reveals vagueness and equivocation in this distinction. Spatiotemporally located entities are those appearing in box A of Figure 8.5. These may be identified with concreta, defining concreta as those things rigidly constantly dependent on some real entity. All concreta are at least closely associated with a particular spatiotemporal location, namely that of the real entity on which they are constantly dependent. Because, trivially, everything is rigidly constantly dependent on itself, all real objects are concreta.

The issue of where abstracta fall on this system is more tangled, although the entanglement itself is quite revealing.[13] "The abstract" is sometimes used as a synonym for "the ideal," to pick out those entities altogether independent of spatiotemporal objects; certainly the term "abstract" often raises such Platonist associations.[14] Such entities would

126

be located in box D, making it readily apparent that under this conception the abstract and the concrete are far from exhaustive.

Sometimes the abstract is contrasted with the particular, which would enable us to define it quite naturally on the above system as those entities not rigidly dependent on any particular spatiotemporal object. Thus those entities in the chart's bottom row would count as abstract under this conception. Clearly there also remain several intervening categories between the abstract, in this conception, and the concrete.

Perhaps the most common understanding of "the abstract," however, is as the opposite of "the concrete," to designate entities "lacking spatiotemporal properties."[15] If one means that they lack *all* spatiotemporal properties, this makes the entities in boxes B, C, and D abstract. For these entities bear, at most, the relation of mere dependence to spatiotemporal entities, and mere dependence is indifferent to the times at which each entity exists. By contrast, an entity that is historically dependent cannot exist at any time before its supporting spatiotemporal entity exists. Typically, historically dependent entities come into existence at a certain time and thus have a temporal origin, giving them temporal properties even if they lack a definite spatiotemporal location. Again on this conception of the abstract, the concrete and the abstract turn out not to be exhaustive categories.

If, however, we are content to let "abstract" designate entities merely lacking a spatiotemporal location (but perhaps having some temporal properties such as a temporal origin), then we can define "abstracta" as those entities that are not rigidly constantly dependent on any real entity and so lack a spatiotemporal location. This conception is close to the most common understanding of the term "abstract" and makes concreta and abstracta mutually exclusive and exhaustive categories; thus I suggest that we take up this definition of "abstract" in the work that follows. On this view, the lower three rows contain the abstracta; concreta occupy the upper left box of tthe figure. Our ability to isolate these different meanings of "the abstract" and show that they might have different extensions already shows a major problem with basing ontological decisions on unexamined category bifurcations and demonstrates how working with a fine-grained and exhaustive system of categories can help to avoid equivocations and false dichotomies.

UNFAMILIAR CATEGORIES

As we have seen, binary divisions of categories, for example into the real and the ideal or the purely material and the mental, pick out only the extreme cases. The intervening categories are not idle possibilities but instead form the categories that seem to be required to do justice to many sorts of objects in the social and cultural world that do not fit naturally into any of these extremes. Not surprisingly, it is precisely these sorts of entities that are seldom given an adequate ontological analysis.

Because I am here only laying out a categorial ontology, the following remarks should not be taken as arguments that we must postulate the entities under discussion and place them in the category suggested. They should, however, demonstrate the apparent uses of these intervening categories for characterizing a great many everyday objects and provide room to see what would be at stake in admitting or denying them. Whatever settled view one reaches regarding the existence and status of such entities, the decision should not be dictated by the constraints of an inadequate system of categories.

Between the Material and the Mental

There seem to be many objects that are neither mental states nor purely material objects completely independent of the mental. On the contrary, most of the social and cultural world surrounding us seems to lie between these extremes. Most often, what is at issue is the dependence of social and cultural objects not on particular mental states of individuals but rather on social practices and collective intentionality of certain sorts. Indeed recently Searle has argued that social facts are fundamentally those facts involving collective intentionality – shared beliefs, desires, intentions, and so forth regarding the way "we" do things.[16] Mortgages rely on shared agreements and practices regarding housing loans, money on collectively "counting" certain objects as valuable for exchange, government on collective acceptance that certain individuals have the right to behave in certain ways. The dependencies of entities in the social and cultural world on our collective beliefs and practices is thoroughgoing. But although it is ordinarily certain forms of meaningful group behavior on which such entities rely, for there to be meaningful social practices requires in turn that there be agents capable of understanding their world and representing it in certain ways to themselves and others, collectively "counting" entities as money, tools, or contracts, and so on. Thus these practices in turn rely on the existence of agents capable of representing their world, making such social entities, which are immediately dependent on social practices, ultimately dependent on mental states.

Dependence on Mental States

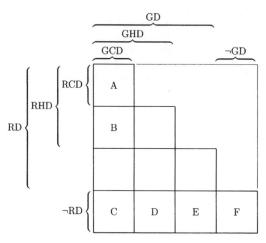

FIGURE 8.6   Categories based in dependence on mental states.

There are many different sorts of mentality-dependent entities, according to the way in which the entity depends on mental states. An entity may be merely dependent on mentality, historically dependent on mental states, or constantly dependent on mental states. (In any of these cases it may also be dependent in any way on spatiotemporal entities). I treat some of the more interesting cases in turn, proceeding from the most to least dependent on mental states.

Mental states themselves and their real contents (like that of John's initial thought that he should quit smoking) are *rigidly constantly dependent* on a particular mental state and so belong in box A of Figure 8.6. Artifacts, although not themselves mental states, are also dependent on mental states. Because "artifact" is generally used to mean a product of human work, "artifacts" may be defined as those entities historically dependent on mental states, placing them in the left two columns of Figure 8.6. Tables and chairs provide classic examples of artifacts. If a piece of chair-shaped wood washes ashore, we would not call it a chair unless we had good reason to believe that it was created by intelligent beings intending it as a seating device; a natural object such as a stump or a piece of driftwood shaped as a chair would not count as a proper chair. Margolis argues that the same applies to works of art: Even a work of painting or sculpture based on one physical entity (canvas, lump of stone) is not identical with the physical object but only embodied in it:

The reason for theorizing thus is, quite simply, that works of art are the products of culturally informed labor and that physical objects are not. So seen, they must possess properties that physical objects, *qua* physical objects, do not and cannot possess. Hence, an identity thesis leads to palpable contradictions. Furthermore, the conception of embodiment promises to facilitate a nonreductive account of the relationship between physical nature and human culture, without dualistic assumptions.[17]

Of these artifacts some, such as works of art, may be rigidly historically dependent on the mental states that create them and continue to depend generically on the presence of agents able to understand them and co-constitute their aesthetic properties (box B, Fig. 8.6).

Other entities may be merely generically dependent on mental states for their origination as well as their preservation. Concrete cultural objects provide many examples of entities generically constantly dependent on mental states. A piece of land only becomes property, or a piece of paper money, through the collective intentional acts of a society that determines to count each as such, but there may be no particular intentional states required to bring each into existence.[18] Laws of state may provide examples of abstract cultural objects merely generically historically dependent on mental states. In at least one sense, if we speak of two states having the same law, or contrast cases in which one law is expressed in several different statutes at different times and places, we seem to treat laws of state as entities that could be brought into existence by any number of different mental states. For although a law does not exist unless it is brought into existence by acts of writing, raising hands, or marking ballots (each of which, to be a genuine piece of voting behavior, requires that it be done with the intention of casting a vote), one and the same law might be on the books even if it were drafted and approved by different groups of legislators. This suggests that laws of state are merely generically historically dependent on mental states of a certain variety. In addition, it seems that laws remain constantly generically dependent on the presence of a community in which they are directly accepted as laws (through people believing that this is a law) or indirectly accepted as laws (e.g., through people believing that anything passed by the legislature and remaining on the books is a law, even if no one happens to recall this law). On this analysis, laws would belong in box C of Figure 8.6.

Universals that are kinds of psychic states, if treated on an *in rebus* view of universals such as Armstrong's, would provide candidates for entities that are merely dependent on mental states (and so belong in box E of Fig. 8.6). The universal *delight* for example, would then be said to exist only if there is something, at some time, that instantiates the state of being delighted. Finally, things that are independent of the mental, as basic physical entities are taken to be in a realist view, or as mathematical entities are considered in a Platonist view, would belong in box F. Once again, the fact that mental states themselves and purely material entities occupy only the opposite corners of our diagram of possible categories suggests the mental and the (purely) material are not jointly exhaustive categories; they are merely the extremes between which most familiar entities appear to fall.

Between the Real and the Ideal

There are also many intervening categories lying between those suited for ordinary spatiotemporal particulars and the Platonist's timeless, changeless ideal objects. Many things in the everyday world seem to provide examples of abstract objects that not only exist contingently but must be created. Art objects of various kinds – works of music, literature, visual designs – are good candidates for abstract entities that nonetheless constantly depend generically on some real entities of a certain type and also rigidly depend historically on certain real entities to bring them into existence (Fig. 8.7,

Dependence on Real Entities

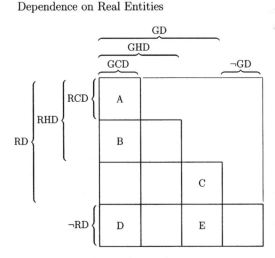

FIGURE 8.7   Categories based in dependence on real entities.

box B).[19] A work of literature like a novel or a poem seems to have no particular location in space and time, although printed copies of it do. A work of literature or music can be realized in more than one real object or performance; there can be many copies of the same narrative. Any particular copy of *Moby Dick* could be destroyed without thereby affecting the work of art *Moby Dick* in the least, neither destroying it (as would be the case if it were identical with this concrete copy) nor diminishing it (as would be the case if it were identical with the manifold of its copies). So although the continued existence of a particular literary work might require that of *some* copy of it, the work is merely generically constantly dependent on some such copy. Consequently, although each copy of the book may have a particular location, the work of literature itself has no spatiotemporal location.

It seems, however, that works of art do come into being at a certain time and are individuated in part by their origin (the circumstances and source of their creation). For example, as I have argued above, if two authors coincidentally write the same words in the same order, they write not one but two literary works. Levinson argues in detail that the same holds of musical works, proposing an analysis of musical works under which not only are they essentially created entities, but "it is logically impossible for a work to have been composed by other than its actual composer."[20] A particular literary or musical work, then, seems to be rigidly historically dependent on the creative (mental and physical) acts of its creator, for it requires these very acts in order to come into existence, and thus, necessarily, if it exists at any time those creative acts must exist at that time or some prior time.

An important subclass of abstracta consists in those entities that are *not* rigidly dependent on anything real. Such abstracta may nonetheless be *generically* dependent on real entities in any way. Visual patterns and melodies, unlike works of art, seem to be merely generically historically dependent abstracta: Although sonatas independently composed by two different individuals must be different works of music, the same melody may appear in both works, suggesting that melodies are not rigidly historically dependent on the acts that produce them. Yet it still seems more natural to treat melodies as created rather than discovered; it seems only those with a Platonist ax to grind would consider a melody to exist before it is ever written or played, and so they do seem to be historically dependent entities (although only generically so). What goes for works of art seems to go for a wide range of other social and cultural entities

132

such as computer programs and laws of state, neither of which is identifiable with any particular instantiation of it on disk or paper, and both of which must be created (programmed, voted on) to come into existence. It would be not only wrong but absurd to claim that Windows 95 or drunk driving laws had always existed.

It seems similarly odd to claim that a technologically invented kind, such as the telephone, has always existed.[21] Thus inventions (the types) seem to provide good candidates for abstract entities that are generically historically dependent on real acts, belonging in box D of Figure 8.7. It seems that they are historically dependent, for it seems legitimate to claim that the telephone did not exist before the mid-1800s – before then, one might say, there was no such kind of thing, and it took human inventiveness (drawing plans, making prototypes) to bring this kind of thing into existence. Nonetheless, a telephone is defined by its functional properties rather than its genetic lineage; many different people could invent the very same kind of machine, provided it served the same sort of function by the same sort of means. In fact, in the case of the telephone, many people did invent it independently: Before Alexander Graham Bell's patent was issued, telephones had been independently produced by both Philipp Reis and Elisha Gray, and at least eight other people had worked out the idea.[22] Thus, although it took the creativity of someone *like* Bell to create the type of machine known as a telephone, the existence of the telephone does not depend on Bell's existence in particular, nor on his acts of invention. This suggests that technological kinds are generically, not rigidly, historically dependent on mental states, for they merely require the performance of *some* real activities of the right kind in order to come into existence. Nonetheless, such technological types, it seems, might fall out of existence if they go out of production and all examples of them and plans for them cease to exist, making such types generically constantly dependent on real things of a certain kind. Making sense of the social world again requires that we break out of traditional category bifurcations into the real and the ideal to acknowledge a variety of contingent, dependent abstracta.

Even those who conceive of all properties as universals on an Aristotelian or Armstrongian model need the space in between the real and the ideal to accommodate properties. On such views, universals are often characterized as dependent merely on being instantiated *at any time* (past, present, or future), so that redness, for example, exists if and only if there is some time t, and some individual a, such that a is red at t.[23] This involves treating universals as generically dependent abstracta, belonging in box E of Figure 8.7. As abstracta, such universals could not themselves be said to have a spatiotemporal location even though they might be generically dependent only on real particulars. This suggests a way of resolving the long-standing problem about the "location" of universals in space-time, for naturalism may be reconciled with the view that universals have no single or multiple location provided that the naturalist accepts not only spatiotemporal entities but also those things dependent (only) on them.[24]

By the same token, Armstrong's impure types – types "logically tied to a certain particular" such as *being the wife of Henry VIII* – would belong in box C, as entities rigidly dependent on (but not rigidly historically dependent on) a particular real entity.[25] As with other universals, on an *in rebus* view these might be said to exist just in case, for example, something, at some time, instantiates the property of being the wife of Henry VIII. Such universals are merely dependent (not historically dependent or constantly dependent), but this dependence is rigid dependence on a particular individual, namely Henry VIII, existing at some time or other.

In addition to showing up the space of possibilities lying between traditional category bifurcations, this system of categories also makes evident the variety of combinations that are possible across the two axes of classification. In principle, at least, it seems possible for there to be all manner of combinations; thus, for example, there may be concrete entities that depend on mental states (e.g., the White House, the *Mona Lisa*, this dollar bill) or concrete entities independent of the mental (e.g., rocks, molecules, stars). By the same token, there may be abstract entities dependent on the mental (e.g., computer programs, symphonies, laws) as well as abstracta independent of the mental (e.g., universals of mass or length, numbers in a Platonist view). By working from a multidimensional system of categories we are able to draw out the full space of possibilities that seem to be needed to accommodate a great variety of entities. Whether or not one ultimately accepts that these categories are filled, the categories at least provide the space to argue the question sensibly and to see what is at stake in postulating entities that fall between the cracks of traditional category systems.

A TOOL FOR ONTOLOGY

The multidimensional system of categories outlined should help avoid the sources of skepticism about categories and thereby clear the way for bringing categories back as a multifaceted tool for ontology. The category system outlined has a number of potential applications. First, it provides a scheme for comparing different ontologies in terms of the types of purported entities they would eliminate or admit. A strict materialist, for example, would eliminate everything not in the lower right box of Figure 8.6. A Berkeleyan idealist, claiming that everything constantly depends on the mental (but perhaps on no particular mental states) would claim that only the far left column of Figure 8.6 was occupied. A nominalist concerned to do without all non–space-time-located entities (not just to do away with classes or universals) would eliminate everything not in box A of Figure 8.7.

A second interesting result is that many traditional pairs of categories are not jointly exhaustive, for intermediate categories may be distinguished. The intervening categories provide alternatives wherein new resolutions to old conflicts may be sought. For example, realist and intuitionist views of mathematical entities represent mathematical entities as being in box F of Fig. 8.6 (independent of the mental) and box D (generically historically dependent on mental states of a certain variety), respectively. But simply locating these views on our category system makes another alternative apparent (box E): That mathematical entities are dependent on the mental (so that a world without agents capable of thought is a world without mathematical objects) but not created by it. Similar considerations apply to debates between Platonists and constructivists about the status of moral values: One need not take the view that values are independent of mental states or the human world to avoid the Sartrean position that values are created by our choices (and so historically dependent on them). Breaking out of the constraints of traditional category bifurcations makes the variety of possible resolutions to ontological difficulties apparent, enabling us to avoid being taken in by the false dichotomies generated by inadequate systems of categories.

Discovering intervening categories also enables us to do greater justice to the status of entities that fall between the cracks of traditional category systems. Binary divisions of categories, for example into the real and the ideal or the purely material and the mental, only pick out the extreme cases. The world seems to be far more varied than these divisions would allow. Indeed many sorts of objects in our environment, from persons to tools to works of art, social institutions, and scientific theories, do not fit naturally into any of these extremes. Whatever settled view we reach regarding the status of these entities, surely we would not want our decision to be made for us simply because we lack an exhaustive system of categories. Laying out a fine-grained and exhaustive system of categories may uncover new categories better suited for characterizing certain types of entities and provide a way out of the ruts of old debates based on false dichotomies.

But the most important use of these categories is that they provide the means for making clear, consistent, and thorough ontological decisions. First, they enable us to make principled and sweeping (rather than piecemeal) decisions by determining which of the categories are occupied and which empty. By making the connections among entities in different categories evident, the categories also enable us to avoid making arbitrary or inconsistent decisions about what to admit. Second, because we can locate purported entities on our charts before we decide whether or not to say there are such things, the categories aid us in deciding whether to admit entities of a particular kind, such as fictional objects or universals, by making visible the costs and benefits of eliminating such entities, given our other commitments. It is time to apply this tool to the case of fictional objects and to examine what the costs and benefits might be of eliminating them from our ontology.

9

Perils of False Parsimony

The lure of parsimony lies behind many ontological decisions. In this respect the case of fictional objects is not unique, for the desire for a thriftier ontology forms the most important motivation for rejecting fictional characters. As a result, a great deal of philosophical ingenuity is expended trying to analyze away apparent reference to fictional objects, to show how we can avoid having fictional objects "forced on" us by talking instead of works of literature or games of make-believe.

Despite the centrality of concerns of parsimony in shaping ontologies, claims to parsimony are often invoked without any analysis of the concept of ontological parsimony and without any attempt to distinguish genuine from false parsimony. But even in the literal use of the term "parsimony" to mean running a household economically, we all recognize (or learn to recognize) the difference between genuine parsimony and false parsimony. You do not run a more parsimonious household just by refusing to buy anything – what you need is an overall plan in terms of which you can see the long-range effects of your purchasing and try, in the long term, to get more for less.

Although the principles for parsimony of a philosophical theory are different from those of household parsimony, it is still important to distinguish genuine parsimony from false parsimony in philosophical theories. Just as we do not necessarily run a more parsimonious household by refusing to buy anything, simply eliminating entities wherever possible does not inevitably result in a more parsimonious ontology. Laying out a parsimonious ontology, too, requires the context of an overall plan or large-scale ontological picture, as indiscriminate elimination on a piecemeal basis can actually interfere with the formulation of a smooth and consistent theory.

The call to parsimony finds its most famous statement in Ockham's razor: It is vain to do with many what can be done with fewer. But this should not be misunderstood as a simple incitement to deny entities wherever possible. Naturally a slimmer ontology is preferable only if one can do everything with the fewer entities that one could do with more. In the case of fiction, for example, this would mean that we would have to be able to offer an equally good account of fictional discourse and the apparent experiences of fictional objects simply in terms of literary works. I have already suggested that I find such prospects dubious. But I leave aside those issues for the moment and ask instead, supposing one could do without fictional objects (in favor of works of literature, games, etc.), would this be more parsimonious? I argue that it would not, that the elimination of fictional objects in favor of literary works or games is a paradigm case of false parsimony.

GENUINE PARSIMONY VERSUS FALSE PARSIMONY

To properly interpret Ockham's razor, we need to know what counts as many and what as fewer. There seem to be at least three types of cases in which eliminating entities does not yield a more parsimonious ontology. First, if ontological parsimony is concerned, it seems clear that it is not numbers but kinds of entities postulated that is at issue. We would gain no real simplicity by rejecting baseball games but accepting board games into our ontology, because they are entities of the same basic type, sharing the same relevant characteristics (being events that occur over time, governed by certain publicly agreed-on rules, engaged in by agents as "players," etc.). Rejecting some entities but accepting others of the same kind is the first type of false parsimony. Although no one would seriously defend an ontology that accepted one kind of game and rejected another, those who adopt a "piecemeal Platonism," accepting some ideal entities while rejecting others, present such a case of false parsimony.[1]

One similarly reaps only a false parsimony by arbitrarily singling out entities in a single category for rejection but retaining entities in other categories with relevantly similar characteristics. Selecting out a single category, such as universals, for exclusion, but retaining other abstract entities dependent on real objects, such as theories and works of art, would (if the above classifications of these entities are correct) be offering a false parsimony of the second type.

The way to approach genuine theoretical parsimony is in terms of a smooth overarching theory of what sorts of entities we should accept, utilizing a minimal number of basic entities, not by singling out particular categories of entities to reject. Consider the genuine parsimony gained when it was discovered that all of the basic chemical elements in the periodic table could be understood much more simply in terms of different combinations of protons, neutrons, and electrons, so that instead of postulating dozens of basic chemical elements we could analyze them all in terms of combinations of three more basic kinds of entities. One could not make that theory more parsimonious by claiming that some particular element, say plutonium, did not exist, and by trying to rephrase all of our apparent talk about plutonium in terms of other things. That would only disturb the elegance and simplicity of the theory, not make it more parsimonious, for the basic entities and ways of combining them remain the same. Eliminating top-level categories of entities that can be accounted for in terms of basic elements that remain is a third variety of false parsimony. Genuine parsimony comes not from rejecting just any sort of entity but rather from minimizing commitments to the relevant ontological kinds of entities based on the principles of a smooth and elegant theory that, among other things, says what the most basic entities are and how they can be combined.

IS DOING WITHOUT FICTIONAL OBJECTS REALLY MORE PARSIMONIOUS?

Should we postulate fictional objects or eliminate them in the interests of parsimony? At first glance it might seem as if fictional characters and works of literature are categorically different entities – that literary works are linguistic and fictional works are imaginary people or some such. As philosophers, we have been relatively at home in dealing with language for some time, so literary works are likely to seem familiar and easy to analyze. Imaginary people, on the other hand, seem a very odd sort of thing liable to invite all manner of confusions. It is, perhaps, reasoning along these lines that has supported the general assumption that we can offer a more parsimonious theory by eliminating fictional characters in favor of literary works. But it is time to examine matters more closely. What is a linguistic entity such as a literary work, and what are fictional characters?

I have been arguing that fictional characters are not to be understood as people – nonexistent, imaginary, or otherwise – but as cultural creations, abstract artifacts produced through intentionality and requiring concrete entities such as copies of stories and a capable readership to go on existing. Literature and language itself, too, are surely (I would argue) abstract cultural creations *par excellence*. They are cultural creations of a representational kind, making use of meaningful symbols – symbols endowed with meaning through our individual or collective intentional acts – to represent something beyond themselves. Indeed, because of its representational capacity, language is that cultural entity that makes other cultural entities such as literary works and fictional characters possible.[2] Put in those terms, it may quickly become less obvious that fictional characters and literary works belong in entirely different categories.

We can address more precisely the question of whether doing without fictional objects is really more parsimonious by making use of the procedure described above. I take the question in two steps: First by seeing where fictional objects, as described in Chapter 1, would fall on the category system outlined in Chapter 8, and then by analyzing the potential costs and benefits of eliminating them. In Part One standard objections to postulating fictional objects, based on fears that so doing would lead to problems with reference or trouble with individuation, are defused. If those arguments are correct, then such worries give us no reason to reject fictional objects, and so we may consider parsimony to be the major issue remaining in deciding whether or not to postulate fictional objects. In particular, we may focus on the question of whether or not eliminating them in favor of literary works and games would provide a more parsimonious ontology.

If we postulated fictional objects, what would they be? I argue in Chapter 1 that if we are to postulate fictional objects at all we should consider them to be entities that satisfy or make sense of our ordinary beliefs and practices regarding them. One important feature of our characterization of fictional characters lies in treating them as created entities, in effect as entities rigidly historically dependent on the real activities and intentional representations of the author who created them.[3] Thus they belong somewhere in the upper two rows of Figure 9.1. Although fictional characters are rigidly historically dependent on some particular real activities, it seems that there is no single real entity on which the continued existence of fictional characters depends. Moreover, although no particular real object such as a particular copy of the book or an utterance is necessary for the character's ongoing existence, it does seem that a fictional character is at least generically constantly dependent on there being *some* copy of a literary work in which it appears. Thus, if we take our apparent experiences and practices about fictional characters, their identity conditions, and their survival seriously, it seems that the category

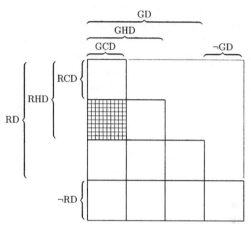

FIGURE 9.1   Fictional characters, categorized by dependencies on real entities.

that would be most natural for entities that would satisfy these practices would be the shaded box of Figure 9.1.

This category is not only the one suitable for fictional objects, however – our discussion in the previous chapter suggested that this is also the category appropriate for works of literature and music. It is often assumed that literary works are something that we understand immediately and nonproblematically, so that a great advance is made if we can rephrase our apparent talk about fictional characters in terms of talk about the literary works in which they appear. Yet the status of a literary work is hardly more readily understood than that of a fictional character, and indeed the two share many features. I argue in previous chapters that although the continued existence of a particular work of literature requires that of some copy of it, a work of literature or music can be realized in more than one real object or performance; there can be many copies of the same narrative, so a work of literature, like a fictional character, is merely generically constantly dependent on some real entity. I have also argued above that a literary work is rigidly historically dependent on the acts of the author that bring it into existence, so in short, a literary work is an abstract entity generically constantly dependent and rigidly historically dependent on real entities. Works of literature seem to bear just the same sorts of dependence relations to real entities that fictional characters do, and so seem to belong in just the same ontological category as the characters they are supposed to replace in allegedly more parsimonious theories.

Although we have located fictional characters on our first category scheme regarding their dependencies on real (spatiotemporal) entities, we have not yet considered where fictional characters would fall on the second category scheme, regarding their dependencies on mental states. As I argue in previous chapters, however, a fictional character comes into existence (if at all) only through the creative acts of an author, and the character created depends rigidly on these creative acts. These creative acts must involve intentionality as well as some real physical activities. Merely physical acts and events are not enough to generate a fictional character. Once again, it seems that a literary work is in just the same position as a fictional character, for it, too, is historically dependent on mental states. A literary work only comes into existence through the intentional mental states of an author; if a pile of sticks happens to wash up on shore arranged into what looks like a series of letters at the water's edge, we have a remarkable occurrence, but not a work of literature, nor any fictional characters, but only some marks that happen to resemble letters and words. So the creative acts from which fictional characters and literary works alike are generated, it seems, must involve intentionality and so are dependent on the mental. Therefore, both fictional characters and works of literature belong somewhere in the upper two rows of Figure 9.2.

In virtue of their ongoing dependence on a capable readership, literary works as well as the fictional characters appearing in them are not only

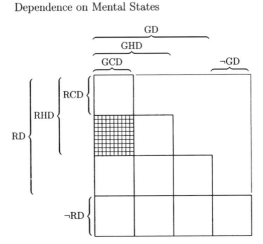

Dependence on Mental States

FIGURE 9.2   Fictional characters, categorized by dependencies on mental states.

historically dependent on but also constantly dependent on mental states, and so belong in the shaded box of Figure 9.2, as entities rigidly historically dependent on and generically constantly dependent on mental states. Thus the category suitable for fictional characters turns out on both sides, with regard to dependencies on real entities and on mental states, to be identical with that suitable for literary works.

It is worth noting that one need not even accept the above category system to arrive at the same conclusion, for fictional characters and literary works (under the analyses I have suggested) would land in the same category according to other major category systems as well. In formal divisions of categories into objects, properties, relations, and states of affairs, both would belong among the objects; if one divides things simply into the abstract and concrete, both are abstract; if one divides things into the contingent and the necessary, both are contingent.

We can now answer the question I posed at the beginning of this chapter: Is doing without fictional objects really more parsimonious? The answer is, no, not as such. Those who "do without" fictional objects almost without exception rely heavily on the notion of a literary work in order to avoid apparent references to fictional objects. But if one keeps works of literature, then one gains nothing but false parsimony by "getting rid of" fictional objects, for they are in just the same categories, and so this is no more "parsimonious" than rejecting baseball games and accepting board games into our ontology. At bottom, despite the fact that literary works are "made up" of words and fictional characters are not, both are abstract cultural creations depending on mental states of certain types. So, as we might have expected; if you have literary works, the characters in them come along with them. Eliminating fictional characters in favor of literary works is thus a classic case of false parsimony of the first kind. So it seems that philosophical ingenuity is better spent elsewhere than in rewriting apparent talk about fictional objects in terms of talk about works of literature. The challenge for those who still maintain that it is worthwhile to reject fictional objects in favor of works of literature is to find the relevant ontological difference between them.

One might try to gain parsimony by eliminating or reducing all entities in this category, including fictional characters, literary works, musical works, and so on. Doing so would make it still more difficult to offer a good account of fictional discourse and our experience of fictional objects, for explanations in terms of works of literature would then be unavailable. But regardless of whether or not a plausible account could be offered, singling out this one category for elimination would be of no advantage. False parsimony occurs not only if some objects in a particular category are excluded and others included, but also if a single category is arbitrarily singled out for exclusion but others with the same relevant characteristics are retained. Those who accept some abstract entities merely generically constantly dependent on real entities, such as scientific theories, universals, numbers, and works of art; and some entities constantly dependent on mental states, including churches, psychological states, governments and laws of state, would gain no genuine parsimony by rejecting all members of the category in which fictional characters and literary works appear (the category of entities generically constantly dependent on both mental states and real entities). In fact, it would seem an arbitrary whim, and a case of false parsimony of the second kind, to single out that category for exclusion, for this is simply the case in which these characteristics are combined.[4] This should serve as a general warning about the dangers of approaching ontology in a piecemeal manner, applying the need criterion to different groups of entities without first undertaking the steps of formulating a general category system and determining where different sorts of entities would fall on it.

No doubt it is possible to formulate a more parsimonious theory that eliminates fictional objects. One could, for example, eliminate all entities that are dependent on the mental – or even just entities that depend on mental states but are not identical with mental states. This is a properly general principle addressing a relevant characteristic and gets rid of fictional objects. But it also eliminates a wide range of other entities. For, if our initial categorization is correct, such things as works of art and scientific theories, churches and schools, and behaviors and social institutions depend on mental states just as fictional objects do, so to take this genuinely parsimonious alternative, one must be willing to do away with that whole range of entities and find some way of accounting for our apparent experiences of and talk about them. One can eliminate fictional objects on the grounds of their dependence on the mental only if one is willing to strip the ontological landscape of this variety of entities as well.

Or one could eliminate on principle anything that is not concrete – that is not rigidly constantly dependent on any single spatiotemporal entity. This, again, is genuinely parsimonious but involves giving up a lot more than fictional objects. For abstractness is by no means a feature unique to fictional objects; indeed many more respectable purported entities lack stronger connections to real, spatiotemporal entities than those fictional objects enjoy. Like fictional objects, ideal entities like numbers

(Platonistically conceived) and abstract entities like universals, laws, and scientific theories, are not rigidly constantly dependent on any real object and so fail to be located in space–time. They, too, are abstract.

In either case, the costs of this parsimony are high, and the defender of either of these alternatives will have to show that we *can* do without entities of all of these kinds, so we do not need to postulate them. This, I suggest, will be a very difficult task. In short, fictional objects turn out not to be such strange creatures after all but instead to share their most important features with many different types of entities in the everyday world. Their dependence on the mental characterizes an entire range of cultural entities, and their abstractness is common to entities from theories to universals to laws. Given their strong similarities to these more accepted entities, those who persist in singling out fictional objects for rejection may be left with no more justification than that of prejudice and tradition, and those who wish to reject fictional objects on general principles may find themselves rejecting far more than they had bargained for.

This should serve as a general warning about the dangers of approaching ontology in a piecemeal manner, asking individually whether we should admit entities of different kinds into our ontology without using general principles for rejecting and accepting entities. For without such a generalized approach, we may end up expending a lot of philosophical energy, with only the result of offering an ontology that is no more parsimonious, and at the cost of losing a unified ontological picture.

10

Ontology for a Varied World

It is time to turn to the second ontological task, offering an assessment of what there is. We can already draw some conclusions from the ways in which our categories are drawn out and from their relations to each other. First, if we take our ordinary beliefs and practices at face value, then it seems that a great proportion of entities including scientific theories, works of art, and cultural artifacts do not fit easily into traditional categories such as the real and the ideal, the material and the mental. Thus we either have to show that we can eliminate or reduce all of these to objects lying in the traditional categories or postulate a richer ontology able to account for such variation.

Second, because of the close relations among the categories, questions of whether or not to postulate many sorts of entity hang together. Thus the stakes are high, for despite the apparent variety of entities, principled decisions to eliminate one type of entity may have wide-ranging consequences. For example, consistency requires that if you eliminate the supporting entities such as mental states, you eliminate all of those cultural objects, behaviors, and institutions that depend on intentionality. If you eliminate abstract objects on principle, you find poems and sonatas, laws and theories disappear along with your rejected universals. And if you eliminate fictional objects but keep stories or other abstract entities depending on mental states, you are left with a theory that has only false parsimony.

A central moral of this study has been that if you treat fictional characters as cultural creations, their fate and their problems hang together with much of the rest of the everyday world, making fictional characters a test case and enabling work on them to provide the beginnings in the much larger struggle to devise an adequate ontology of the everyday world. But if the fate of fictional objects hangs together with that of a range of other everyday entities, what should we do with them all? How can we account for the variety that characterizes the everyday world without losing the ability to offer an elegant and unified view of what there is? Let us once again address this large issue by starting from the revealing case of fictional objects.

LESSONS FROM THE CASE OF FICTION

Earlier I postponed the issue of whether we should postulate fictional objects, beginning instead by asking what they would be if we were to postulate them, whether so doing would bring us into any difficulties, and what benefits eliminating them might bring. Now the time has come to face the question. Should we postulate fictional objects? Our results suggest that we should.

In Part I we were able to overcome many standard objections to postulating fictional objects, in particular those based in worries that so doing will bring us into trouble by landing us in contradiction, saddling us with entities that we cannot naturalistically refer to or acquire knowledge of, or burdening our theories with entities that do not admit of clear and sensible identity conditions. Each of these problems proved resolvable by conceiving of fictional characters as abstract artifacts closely tied to entities such as stories, authors, and readers. Thus such apparent barriers to postulating fictional objects proved, on closer examination, to pose no difficulties.

Not only do purported problems give us no reason to reject fictional characters, but we seem to have good reason to accept them in the interests of offering adequate and elegant analyses of language and experience. By postulating fictional characters as the objects of certain intentional experiences, we are able to offer a theory of intentionality that is better able to account for the copresence of distinct features of intentionality in all kinds of intentional acts. By allowing that there are fictional characters to which we can refer we can offer an analysis of fictional discourse that is simple, not ad hoc, and does not confuse issues of semantics and syntax by altering how one reads a sentence based solely on the type of object referred to. Postulating fictional objects thus enables us to offer theories of experience and language that succeed better on their own terms. This gives us prima facie reason to postulate fictional objects.

The major incentive to avoid postulating fictional objects (and that might make many still hesitate to postulate them even if they are convinced

147

of the above advantages) is that of parsimony. But we have also seen that one does not necessarily gain a more parsimonious theory simply by eliminating objects of a given type. Eliminating fictional objects *and* the literary works in which they appear would be, it seems, extraordinarily difficult unless we are willing to completely ignore, discount, or revise our ways of discussing fiction both in the practice of literary criticism and our ordinary lives. But eliminating fictional objects by referring only to the works of literature that support them provides no real parsimony, because the entities are relevantly similar. Although parsimony provides no incentive to eliminate fictional characters, however, the need for a smooth, unified, and non–ad hoc account of our discourse and experience provides a strong incentive to keep them. Thus, on balance, the benefits of postulating fictional objects seem to outweigh the costs, for indeed most of the apparent costs have proven illusory. This, it seems to me, gives us sufficient reason to postulate fictional objects as they are considered in the model presented here – as abstract artifacts dependent on literary works and created by authors.

Apart from the apparent difficulties in handling fictional discourse, which (as I argue in Chapter 7) are easily resolved, the main reason why fictional objects have eluded a fully adequate treatment until now may be that they fall firmly between traditional categories. As they are neither real nor ideal, neither material nor purely mental, none of the readily apparent options about what to do with fictional characters succeeds. Attempts to reduce them to concrete marks on pages, acts of thinking, or independent Meinongian entities are equally doomed to failure, as none of these fit the structure of fictional characters as created abstracta, dependent on both concrete material individuals and on mental states.

Far from being peculiar to fictional objects, however, these problems turn out to be symptomatic of problems with the dominant ways of categorizing things. Although fictional characters are among those entities in the everyday world that do not fit easily into traditional category bifurcations such as the real and ideal, they are by no means isolated in their predicament. Although it has been less noticed, a great range of other entities – perhaps even the majority of entities in our everyday world – fall between the cracks of standard category systems.[1] Other abstract artifacts such as laws, theories, and works of music and literature cannot be forced into the categories of either the real or the ideal without giving up some of their most important characteristics, such as their repeatability and their created status. Nor can they be forced into either the category of mental entities or that of material entities without violating some of our most important beliefs about them, such as that they are not merely the subjective contents of a single mind but are shareable, discussible entities, and that they are not destroyed with any of their written copies. Even concrete artifacts such as sculptures, churches, dollar bills, and pieces of real estate cannot be identified with those real entities on which they depend without missing some of the essential characteristics that distinguish them, as cultural artifacts, from mere physical entities. The failure of standard ontological categories to cope with such a wide range of entities suggests the need for a broader, more varied ontology.

There is a temptation to think that we can avoid facing up to these apparent complexities of the everyday world, because (it is hoped) such entities can ultimately be reduced to or eliminated in favor of more tractable scientific entities. But here our study of fiction should give us pause. Fictional characters have long been taken to be among the most tenuous and suspicious of creatures, and worries that discussing them will bring us into confusion or contradiction have driven philosophers to an intensive struggle to find ways to eliminate fictional characters from our ontology. But even here, where the claims to existence seemed most fragile and the attempts at elimination most diligent, fictional characters have proven very difficult to do without.

There is a certain strategic advantage in starting from the case of fictional characters – for these should present the hardest case to establish that these are tractable entities that we should admit to our ontologies. If it proved so difficult to eliminate talk of fictional entities or reduce them to entities in other categories, how much more difficult might it prove to do so with the works of literature in which they appear, or with the cultural, legal, economic, and social institutions that form the backbone of our society and everyday lives? Questions about what these things are, their identity conditions, and how they may depend on cultural and individual beliefs and practices arise naturally not only in philosophical contexts but also in legal contexts, in directing our interpretive practices, and in the way we talk about and use the objects surrounding us. To give up serious discussion of them would be to give up a great deal. Moreover, some of the tricks that are available to help avoid reference to fictional entities are unavailable in these cases – tricks like paraphrasing talk about them in constructions such as "according to the story." The chances of eliminating reference to all entities in these categories without radically reconstruing our most basic everyday beliefs and practices seem slim indeed.

Why would we want to eliminate or reduce them anyway? One reason lies in worries that they will prove intractable, for example that cultural objects will be unsuited for clear individuation and abstracta ineligible for naturalistic reference. But resolving these problems for fictional objects already suggests that these difficulties are not as great as might have at first appeared and provides an example of how these problems may be resolved for other cultural objects and other abstracta. Another motive may be that we simply did not know what to do with such entities, whereas the categories of physical spatiotemporal entities and ideal entities were relatively familiar. But this problem, too, begins to fade as we see how to account for a variety of objects based on their varying dependencies on spatiotemporal entities and mental states. Although it is too much to establish here, it seems likely that the benefits of postulating these sorts of everyday entities will also outweigh the costs, provided we can find an elegant and relatively parsimonious means of accounting for them.

A MODEST PROPOSAL

The problems with fiction are just the beginning. For it seems a great variety of entities – including a large proportion of objects in the everyday social and cultural world – are unaccounted for among the familiar ranks of the real or ideal, the material or mental. But the fact that the world of our everyday experience seems to include a great variety of entities does not force us to postulate a ragbag ontology stuffed with all sorts of disparate entities, or to abandon all but basic physical entities as part of an intractable mess. For we have the tools to understand the structure of entities of each of these types in terms of their dependencies on spatiotemporal entities and mental states. Moreover, if we do accept fictional objects (on this model), we already are thereby bringing some abstract objects (merely generically dependent on spatiotemporal entities) and some mentality-dependent objects into our ontology and so can admit other such entities without loss of parsimony.

We can account for a great variety of entities (including fictional objects) by adopting a very simple principle: Accept spatiotemporal entities and mental states, and anything that depends (in any way) only on entities that we accept. The first clause ensures that we have room for physical entities and intentionality. The latter clause enables us to account, first, for abstracta merely generically dependent on spatiotemporal entities, such as universals of basic physical kinds; second, for entities dependent – at least immediately – only on mental states, such as intentional mental events themselves, imaginary or hallucinated objects, or universals of types of mental state; and finally for jointly dependent entities such as governments and monuments, songs, theories, literary works, and fictional characters, as well as any higher-level entities, such as aesthetic properties, that may be based on them. The resulting picture is one of the everyday world as the common product of spatiotemporal reality and the creative power of human intentionality – whether in the form of the thoughts of individuals or the joint practices and beliefs of a culture. The vast majority of familiar entities are those that depend on both spatiotemporal, physical entities and mental states, although they may do so in many different ways: rigidly or generically, constantly or historically, or atemporally dependent. Dependencies of all of these types are included, as are dependencies based in formal, material, and nomological necessities. Together, these tools enable us to provide an ontology able to preserve in all of its fullness and diversity a world composed not merely of particles in the void but also of concrete artifacts from dollar bills to schools to cars, and of equally important abstract artifacts such as laws and literary works, computer programs and symphonies, thus making way for an ontology of the everyday world as well as an ontology of physical science.

Referring to the system of categories outlined in Chapter 8, this picture entails that we allow that there may be entities in any combination of the boxes in Fig. 8.3, with one exception. Those entities that would occupy the lower right box of each diagram, and so be ideal entities independent of both spatiotemporal entities and mental states, are not covered by these criteria. It would be an interesting project to see how much of what ideal entities do philosophically and mathematically could be accomplished with some kind of abstracta as they are conceived here. Thus I remain agnostic about whether or not there are, for example, Platonistically conceived mathematical entities. Several possible avenues for accounting for mathematical entities remain on the above model, and so the question seems best left open for further exploration. If these avenues prove fruitful, that would enable one to maintain the basic metaphysical principle that everything is real, or a mental state, or ultimately dependent only on these.

I argue that the way to approach genuine theoretical parsimony is in terms of a theory of what the basic entities are and how they may be combined. On this proposal, the "basic" entities are spatiotemporal entities and mental states. Although I lay out spatiotemporal entities and mental states as the "basic" entities in this picture in the sense that they act as the supporting entities for everything else, however, I do not wish to preclude the possibility that these may, in turn, be analyzable in simpler terms, just as some of the "basic" components behind the periodic chart – protons and neutrons – have proven to be further analyzable. Of course the question of the relation between spatiotemporal entities and mental states brings us at once into the classic problem of the relation between mental and physical entities. We can remain agnostic about this issue for the present. But it is interesting to note that if mental states turn out to be best characterized as (perhaps nomologically) ultimately dependent only on particular spatiotemporal events, we could maintain the principle that everything ultimately depends only on spatiotemporal entities.[2] Since formal, material, and nomological dependencies are included, starting from independent physical particles as our basis, we could include all of those mereological combinations formally constructable out of them and dependent only on them, as well as higher-order biological organisms materially dependent on a physical basis, along with psychological processes and mental states nomologically dependent on physical properties of particular types. From there we could include once again all of those entities with dependencies on the mental as well as on the physical. But whether this further move can be made successfully must be left for further investigation.

Accepting an ontology including mental states, spatiotemporal entities, and the great variety of things built up between them has the advantage of enabling us not only to account for elements of the world of physics, but also for those of the social and cultural world in which we live, which are the objects of the vast majority of our daily thoughts, activities, and discussions. And we can account for each of these in ways that correspond to most of our ordinary beliefs and practices about them, thus eliminating the need to reinterpret or abandon our talk about entities such as works of literature, social collectives, or monetary systems. So the claims in Chapter 8 about what works of art, laws, and artifacts *seemed* to be like can be taken at face value, for those entities can be located precisely in those categories that seemed most natural for them. We need make no attempt to rewrite all of our talk about works of music and their aesthetic qualities in terms of vibrations of particles, to resolve our talk about nations into talk about individual people, or to paraphrase all statements about fictional objects into statements about stories or games. Although certain points may arise at which we may be forced to give up or reinterpret such basic beliefs and practices, it is mere thrill-seeking to throw away central elements of our ordinary beliefs and practices unnecessarily, and such abandonment or revision would here be groundless, because we have the tools we need to account for these entities as they are given to us.

Moreover, because it is based on a fine-grained categorization of different types of dependence, this proposal offers a far greater variety of categories than traditional schemes, enabling us to do justice to the important differences among entities in disparate categories instead of trying to reduce them all to one or two basic types. These fine differences enable us to explain, for example, how literary works differ from types of invention, for we are able to distinguish those entities that depend rigidly on a particular origin (and so are individuated in part on that basis) and those that might be created by a number of different entities. The difference between natural objects and concrete artifacts such as tools and churches is preserved in the difference between those entities dependent and independent of the mental. And we can distinguish between eternal abstracta such as universals and abstract artifacts that, although they lack a spatiotemporal location, do have a temporal origin, namely, the time at which they were created. But we maintain a fine-grained variety in our categories without just positing an ontology stuffed with a jumble of disparate entities. One of the most interesting things about this schema is that it reveals how closely all of these entities are related to each other, both by their interdependencies and by similarities in the ways in which they are dependent.

Perhaps most surprisingly, we can do all of this on a relatively parsimonious basis, for just as the various elements of the periodic table came to be understood in terms of different combinations of three basic sorts of entities, we can account for all of these varied sorts of entities – including fictional objects – by simply accepting real, spatiotemporal objects, mental states, and things that depend on them in various ways. On this view, fictional characters turn out simply to provide particularly interesting examples of abstract entities dependent on both physical entities and mental acts.

Thus the problems of fictional objects turn out not to be strange but strangely significant, and the resolution to the status of fictional objects paves the way for a more comprehensive and finer-grained ontological picture. In fact, this proposal presents an ontological bargain: For the cost of accepting two basic types of entities and those entities that are built up between them, we gain a pay-off not only of a more refined and richer set of categories, but also of the ability to make a far better account of our experience of all kinds of objects in the world around us. Perhaps it is in getting a lot for a little, rather than in pure austerity, that true economy lies.

Notes

1. As I use the term, I do not mean to limit fictional characters to the people said to take part in the story; fictional animals, inanimate objects, events, and processes share the same status and the same analysis. Focusing on the case of literary fictions enables the discussion to be more precise and detailed. But I do not mean to rule out the possibility that there may be something like a fictional character appearing in a painting, in imagination, or even in a hallucination, and the theory developed here should suggest how to handle those cases as well. I simply do not presuppose that the issues in these cases are exactly the same, or that the theory developed automatically applies to these so-called fictional or imaginary entities as well.

2. It is also telling that Roget's *Thesaurus* lists "product" as its first meaning under the heading "fiction," again pointing to the idea that fictional characters are things produced.

3. Here again I am speaking specifically of the characters *qua* literary fictions and do not mean to rule out that characters can also appear in movies, paintings, or acts of imagination. The conditions under which the same character can appear represented via other media would need to be drawn out separately but should proceed along the same lines as those for transtextual character identity, which are drawn out in Chapter 5.

4. More precise conditions regarding whether we can say that one and the same character appears in two or more stories are developed in Chapter 5.

5. Levinson (*Music, Art, and Metaphysics*, 68–73) offers parallel arguments that a musical work is not identical with a pure sound structure.

6. Any discomfort with the idea that fictional characters can cease to exist probably stems from discomfort with admitting that they ever existed at all. In Chapter 7 I discuss how to interpret claims that fictional characters do not exist.

7. The possibility always remains, however, that these stories, and the characters represented in them, may be brought back on the basis of these texts if the language is once again discovered and understood. That one and the same

character or story may exist, cease to exist, and exist once more is not so strange. Given that fictional characters and stories are not spatiotemporally located entities, there seems no reason to require spatiotemporal continuity as an identity condition.

8. Naturally that memory must be by a comprehending individual. If someone merely memorizes the right sounds in the right order without understanding their meaning, a comprehending audience is required in addition to the memory of sounds.

9. Precise identity conditions for stories are laid out in Chapter 5.

10. Bach and Harnish (*Linguistic Communication*, 113–115) discuss such "effective" linguistic acts and the institutional states of affairs they produce.

11. Searle, *Construction of Social Reality*, 74.

12. My own view is that it overstates the case to claim that all institutional facts can exist only if they are represented as existing. Institutional facts, I would say, depend on intentionality but not always on our representing those facts as being the way that they are. A recession, for example, depends on economic systems that depend on human intentionality, but we can be in a recession even if no one represents us as being in a recession. In any case, however, Searle is certainly right that many institutional facts may be brought into existence by being represented as existing and require representations for their existence. It is that common feature that it is important to draw out here.

13. In Chapter 6 I develop and defend the *intentional object theory of intentionality*, according to which every intentional act has a content and an object. It is this creative capacity of intentionality, to make an object if there is none referred to, that guarantees the availability of an object for all kinds of intentional acts.

14. Further discussion of the human world as one dependent on intentionality may be found in my work (Thomasson, "Ontology").

15. See, e.g., Margolis "Ontological Peculiarity," 257–259. Other arguments that at least some works of art are not physical entities may be found in Wollheim, *Art and Its Objects*, sections 4–10; Ingarden, *Literary Work of Art*, sections 2–5; and Wolterstorff, *Worlds of Art*, 42.

16. For discussion of such institutional facts and argument that they depend on human agreement, see Searle, *The Construction of Social Reality*.

17. See Chapters 5, 4, and 7 (respectively) for discussion of how the artifactual theory handles these issues and why its solution presents advantages over Meinongian theories.

18. My criticisms of such theories do not concern their suitability for handling other abstract objects or so-called nonexistents, and in fact theories such as Parsons's and Zalta's have a variety of interesting and fruitful applications. I only claim that these abstract or nonexistent entities are not suited to do the job of handling fictional characters.

19. For Parsons there is exactly one object correlated with each combination of nuclear properties; some of these are real and some nonexistent. For Zalta there is exactly one *abstract* object that *encodes* each combination of properties. In addition, for some combinations of properties there is also an ordinary object

exemplifying exactly those properties. The original such principle may be found in Meinong's *Über Möglichkeit und Wahrscheinlichkeit*, 282; for Parsons see *Nonexistent Objects*, 19; for Zalta see *Abstract Objects*, 12.

20. Zalta's formalized theory of abstract objects admits of two possible interpretations. According to the first, Meinongian, interpretation the quantifier ranging over abstract objects asserts only that "there is" such an object, leaving abstract objects as Meinongian nonexistents. According to the second, Platonist, interpretation, the quantifier may be read as "there exists" even if ranging over abstract entities. Thus it is only under the first interpretation that Zalta's theory shares this common characteristic of Meinongian theories. See Zalta, *Abstract Objects*, 50–52; *Intensional Logic*, 102–104.

21. This is the so-called principle of independence formulated by Meinong's student Ernst Mally. For discussion see Lambert's *Principle of Independence*.

22. For a more detailed discussion of the differences between two-types-of-property views and two-types-of-predication views and how each handles the problems of fictional predication, see Chapter 7.

23. In the Platonist interpretation, Zalta's theory does not share this characteristic, as it asserts the existence of abstract objects. The availability of two different interpretations of Zalta's theory, one of which claims existence for abstract objects and the other of which does not, is a further sign that – provided one admits that there are such objects – the issue of whether or not one is willing to say that they *exist* is primarily one of labeling.

24. This follows from Zalta's (*Abstract Objects*, 91–92) definitions of stories and fictional characters.

25. Parsons, *Nonexistent Objects*, 188.

26. See Chapters 3, 5, and 7.

27. Kripke, "Semantical Considerations," 65 (see also his retraction, 172). Plantinga considers and argues against this case for the existence of unactualized possibilia (*Nature of Necessity*, 153 ff).

28. Versions of this problem are discussed by Kripke (*Naming and Necessity*, 157–158) and by Plantinga (*Nature of Necessity*, 154–155).

29. It does, however, provide a useful contrast case in discussing the place of fictional characters in modal metaphysics, so I return to it briefly in Chapter 3.

30. Crittenden, *Unreality*, 69.

31. van Inwagen, "Creatures of Fiction."

32. The two views also handle predications of fictional objects similarly, although the accounts of the reference of fictional names differ. See Chapters 7 and 4, respectively.

33. van Inwagen, "Creatures of Fiction," 303.

34. Sartre, *Psychology of Imagination*, 177–178.

35. This phrase is borrowed from Wolterstorff, who advances similar criticisms against R. G. Collingwood's treatment of works of art as imaginary entities (Wolterstorff, *Works and Worlds*, 43).

36. Ingarden, *Literary Work of Art*, 117.

37. In Chapter 6 I have more to say about how we can legitimately claim that different readers have experiences of the same fictional character.

CHAPTER 2

1. For a clear and thorough analysis of Husserl's notion of foundation, see Simons, *Philosophy and Logic*, "The Formalization of Husserl's Theory of Wholes and Parts." Important studies of dependence growing out of Husserl's work include Simons's *Parts* and a collection of essays in Smith, ed., *Parts and Moments*.

2. For a discussion of these difficulties, see Fine, "Ontological Dependence," 270–272; Gorman, "Logical and Metaphysical Form."

3. Cases of self-dependence are ruled out by the reference to a "more comprehensive unity" in Husserl's definition of dependence as "A cannot as such exist except in a more comprehensive unity which associates it with an M" (Husserl, *Logical Investigations*, 463). Husserl later allows that we drop the reference to wholes in his definition of dependence, making the definition the more general: A depends on B if and only if "an A can by its essence. . .not exist, unless a B also exists" (476). In his recent theory of dependence based on Husserl's work, Simons works primarily from the former definition and explicitly rules out trivial cases of self-dependence. See, for example his "The Formalization of Husserl's Theory of Wholes and Parts" (Smith, ed., *Parts and Moments*, 124) and his exclusion of the trivial cases of self-dependence in *Parts* (295).

4. Husserl's student Ingarden is the important exception. He develops a theory of dependence that takes time into account by distinguishing derivation, which he defines as an inability to exist unless produced by some other entity, from contingency, which is an inability to go on existing without the support of some other entity (Ingarden, *Time and Modes*). His derivation and contingency are precursors to the notions of historical dependence and constant dependence developed below. For more on Ingarden's pioneering work on dependence, see my work (Thomasson, "Theory of Dependence").

5. For discussion and these examples, see Husserl, *Logical Investigations*, vol. 2, 455–458.

6. Simons's "weak foundation" (*Parts*, 295) is similar to this, with the exception that this definition allows the terms to be objects, states of affairs, or properties; his requires that both terms be individuals.

7. Husserl distinguishes between entities dependent "in the order of coexistence" and those "dependent in the order of succession" (*Logical Investigations*, 460–462). What I call "constant dependence" seems to be what Husserl would call "foundation in the order of coexistence." Husserl's examples of foundation are almost exclusively cases in which the dependence in question is constant, so that A cannot *ever* exist without an M.

8. See Armstrong, *Universals*, 74–75.

9. One could define future dependence in general as: Necessarily, if α exists at t, then β exists at some time after t. Some may object that these examples fail to capture basic properties belonging to the "nature" of a thing, but even if convincing cases are hard to discover, the idea of future dependence is surely at least thinkable.

10. Kripke argues to this effect about Queen Elizabeth (Kripke, *Naming and Necessity*, 110–113).

11. The tan, and any generated property of an object, corresponds to what Ingarden calls an "acquired property" of that object. See Ingarden's discussion of acquired properties (*Der Streit*, vol. II.1, 362–379).

CHAPTER 3

1. These requirements are drawn out more precisely in Chapter 5.
2. Ingarden offers similar arguments (*Literary Work of Art*, 7–19), and Wollheim also argues against identifying literary works with any particular copy or class thereof (*Art and Its Objects*, sections 5–8).
3. Thus by "abstract" here I mean simply lacking a spatiotemporal location. The term "abstract" is used in many different ways; I discuss this problem in Chapter 8.
4. Ingarden argues that literary works cannot be considered as timeless, ideal entities (*Literary Work of Art*, 9–12). Levinson offers similar arguments that a musical work cannot be identified with a mere abstract structure in his "What a Musical Work Is" (Levinson, *Music, Art and Metaphysics*, 65–78).
5. David Armstrong (*Universals*, 75–82) defends an *in rebus* view of universals, arguing that the only universals there are are those instantiated at some time, past, present or future.
6. A clear account of mathematical constructivism may be found in Carl J. Posy, "Brouwer's Constructivism," 125–159.
7. D. W. Smith ("The Background of Intentionality") argues that ideas and intentional contents should be considered dependent, created entities.

CHAPTER 4

1. That is, provided they really are fictional names and do not refer to some real entity (Kripke, *Naming and Necessity*, 24, 157–158). Kripke later acknowledges that although fictional names cannot refer to any actual or possible *person* they may refer to abstract fictional characters. I discuss this briefly subsequently.
2. Crittenden, *Unreality*, 37.
3. This problem leads van Inwagen ("Creatures of Fiction," 307) to suggest that reference by description is the primary means of referring to fictional characters.
4. Regarding mathematical entities, see Benacerraf, "Mathematical Truth."
5. Kripke, *Naming and Necessity*, 23–24.
6. See, for example, Crittenden's and Hunter's arguments that causal-historical theories of reference cannot allow that fictional names refer (Crittenden, *Unreality*, 37; Hunter, "Reference and Meinongian Objects,") Plantinga's arguments that fictional characters cannot be dubbed (*Nature of Necessity*, 155), and van Inwagen's argument that reference by description must be the primary means of referring to fictional characters ("Creatures of Fiction," 307).
7. Speaking of a "naming ceremony" here as in Kripke's account is, admittedly, somewhat simplified and even metaphorical, for it may be that even in standard cases no single event is identifiable as *the* naming ceremony. The means whereby a name is applied to its object, whether in the case of real or fictional entities, may be a long and diffuse process; reference to a particular ceremony is merely a simplified manner of speaking about an ideal case.

8. Zalta ("Referring to Fictional Characters") offers a similar solution, arguing that causal theories of the reference of names can be extended to cover fictional objects, for (provided a wider understanding of baptism) they can be baptized through their stories. His solution does, however, differ from the one here offered in several respects. On his view, a story *in its entirety* functions as an "extended baptism" of a fictional character, so the character cannot be said to be baptized or referred to by the author until after the entire story has been written. This need not be the case in my account: A character may be baptized initially and then referred to by the author who ascribes it new properties later in that or another story. Furthermore, on Zalta's account the referential connection between the story and the character baptized in it is made by a priori metaphysical principles ensuring that each combination of properties described in a story picks out a unique abstract object. In the artifactual theory, it is the chains of dependence between stories and characters that enable us to refer rigidly to a fictional character via a copy of the story, and to maintain that rigid reference even as the properties ascribed to the character evolve through the course of that, or another, story.

9. This points to the role that the background assumptions of readers have in constituting the very plot of a novel. Without some background about, for example, the brands of clothing that a single individual is likely to wear, a reader could not even unify these voices and actions into single characters reidentifiable from chapter to chapter.

10. For details regarding the preservation of a chain of publication of a single story, see Chapter 5.

11. It is interesting to note that these consumers may themselves be sources of *external* but not *internal* information about the character. That is, one may learn who Hamlet is by conversation, never read the play, yet do research to learn outside information about how historical interpretations of him have varied. This information may then be passed along to other members of the naming practice. Although Evans does not make the distinction between inside and outside information, there seems to be a parallel case for real individuals: Someone who had never met Jones, and was hence a consumer in the naming practice, could nonetheless collect outside information about Jones, such as how many times he had been mentioned in the local paper, what his children think of him, and so on, and then pass this information along.

12. Models of cars seem to provide another good example of an abstract artifact, brought into existence at a certain time in particular circumstances. Thus it seems particularly appropriate that these models of car should be referred to directly, by name, rather than by description. A Studebaker is not just any car exhibiting certain design properties, but must have the right history of manufacture following the created plan. Levinson (*Music, Art and Metaphysics*, 81) also discusses models of cars as created, "initiated" types.

13. The problem persists or demands a different solution for any entities conceived as independent abstracta as, for example, mathematical entities are by the Platonist. For one such solution, see Linsky and Zalta, "Naturalized Platonism vs. Platonized Naturalism."

CHAPTER 5

1. Russell, "On Denoting," 205; Quine, "On What There Is," 4.
2. Parsons, *Nonexistent Objects*, 18–19, 188.
3. Zalta, *Abstract Objects*, 13, 93. Although Zalta allows that fictional characters may exemplify certain properties, such as being authored, the properties exemplified play no role in determining their identities.
4. This solution is developed by Wolterstorff (*Works and Worlds*, 144–149) and by Reicher ("Zur Identität fiktiver Gegenstände").
5. Reicher, "Zur Identität fiktiver Gegenstände."
6. Wolterstorff, *Works and Worlds of Art*, 47.
7. Reicher, "Zur Identität fiktiver Gegenstände." This is offered as a supplement to, not a replacement for, Wolterstorff's solution, which is also discussed approvingly there.
8. Note, moreover, that the same problem of cross-textual character identification arises in cases of different editions or translations of a literary work, as well as in different literary works of which one is not a sequel of the other but both are developments of a common myth or legend. So, for a complete theory, we would need identity conditions allowing us to account for all of these. With Reicher, I stick to the issue of sequels here.
9. It must be emphasized that these are offered as sufficient conditions, not necessary conditions for identity: I allow both cases in which one and the same character appears in more than one literary work and cases in which a character may be ascribed different properties, and I discuss such cases in the subsequent section.
10. This condition for appearing in a literary work parallels that offered by Zalta in *Abstract Objects*, 92.
11. What counts as same text type, having the same symbols in the same order, may be semiexplicated as follows: Texts x and y (however brief) are of the same text type if and only if they would be understood as the same by members of the relevant language group in all (even intensional) contexts.
12. I describe only conditions for perfect copies here, because I am laying out sufficient conditions for identity.
13. The claim that background assumptions and language capabilities vary slightly for each individual need not lead us to conclude that each person reads a different literary work. What a literary work typically requires is only a sketchy schema of common knowledge and assumptions combined with enough language capability to understand the literary work; such a schema may certainly be widely shared across different individuals and typically is common to most members of a given culture and language group.
14. As the study of predication in Chapter 7 demonstrates, the fact that a character can be ascribed different properties in different literary works or different editions need not make us worry that identifying such characters violates the principle of the indiscernibility of identicals. For if a character is ascribed conflicting properties in different works, this only shows that the character is such that *according to one work* it is such and such, whereas *according to the other work* it is not.
15. Worries about relying too heavily on authorial intention may be somewhat mitigated by the admission that, as in the examples given previously, the best and most appropriate evidence to use in judging such intentions is that in the text, not that

to be gained by interviewing the author (who may in fact have forgotten or not been explicitly aware of various cultural icons and prior figures that were played on in writing the work). Moreover, this is not a claim about what role the author's intention should play in interpreting the meaning or value of a work, but only a claim that historical facts regarding the author's intention do play a role in determining factual matters such as whether a character is an import or a new creation.

16. The notion of survival is proposed as a more useful notion than identity, and developed in detail by Andrew Brennan (*Conditions of Identity*).

17. Parsons ("Entities without Identity") argues that postulating entities that have certain indeterminate questions regarding their identity does not actually cause the feared problems with quantification it was supposed to. If so, we have all the less reason to let such remaining fuzzy cases prevent us from postulating fictional objects and other entities encountering fuzzy cases.

CHAPTER 6

1. Searle, *Intentionality*; Smith and McIntyre, *Husserl and Intentionality*.

2. I use angle brackets to make it clear that I am speaking of contents.

3. Searle, *Intentionality*, 17.

4. Searle claims this as the "second advantage" of his approach to intentionality (16). See also Sajama and Kamppinen, *Historical Introduction to Phenomenology*, 75.

5. Some of these distinctive features of intentionality and the terminology used to described them are from Smith and McIntyre, *Husserl and Intentionality*, 10–18.

6. For discussion of the twin-earth case vis-à-vis theories of intentionality, see D. W. Smith, "Thoughts."

7. It is in principle no different if we treat intentionality as having the basic structure of a two-term mediated relation (the terms being act and object, mediated by content) or of a three-term relation (act, content, object). I speak in the former manner, as that corresponds more closely to our speech practices: Even if we recognize that content is involved in individuating the relation, the relation of perceiving, for example, is most naturally conceived as a two-term relation holding between act and object via content rather than as a three-term relation involving all of these.

8. Johansson, *Ontological Investigations*, 196–226.

9. For relational versions of a content theory, see Smith and McIntyre, *Husserl and Intentionality*, 10–11; Grossmann, *Categorial Structure*.

10. My "thinking" here should be read as simply placing the objects before the mind, conceiving of them, rather than bearing some propositional attitude towards them.

11. Smith and McIntyre, *Husserl and Intentionality*, 370–371.

12. See, for example, Quine, "On What There Is," 4.

13. See Chapter 1 and Chapter 3 for arguments that fictional characters are rigidly tied to their origin.

14. Cf. Smith and McIntyre, *Husserl and Intentionality*, Chapter 8, in which it is argued that the identity of a natural individual is transcendent in relation to any finite set of contents of acts directed towards it. I suggest we broaden this claim explicitly to include fictional objects as well.

15. Cf. D. W. Smith, *Circle of Acquaintance*, 151–152.

16. This theory has its roots in Twardowski's theory of intentionality, according to which "we must discern, not just a twofold, but a threefold aspect of every presentation: The act, the content and the object" (Twardowski, *Content and Object*, 8). A similar contemporary view is held by Zalta, who defends a Meinongian view that there is always an object of a presentation but combines that with a Husserlian view of contents, so that, in the case of thinking of Pegasus, the thought has both a Husserlian content and is of or about the fictional object Pegasus. (Zalta *Intensional Logic*, 105–114).

17. See Ingarden, *Time and Modes of Being*, 47–52.

18. There are, nonetheless, important differences among purely intentional objects in terms of the types of dependence they exhibit on intentional states, and whether they depend (perhaps mediately) on anything else such as a story.

19. There seems to be no good and sufficiently precise verb for what we do when we picture literary figures to ourselves during the reading process. I call such intentional acts "fictionally seeing," as the fictional counterpart of perceiving or hallucinating. This is, however, not to say that we cannot think of fictional entities unless we are presently reading the relevant book. Just as we cannot only perceive but also remember or imagine a real object, so we cannot only fictionally see but also remember or imagine fictional objects. These acts, however, have a different structure from what I here call fictionally seeing intentional acts.

20. For a discussion of the element of indexicality in intentional contents, see D. W. Smith, *The Circle of Acquaintance*, Chapter 4.

CHAPTER 7

1. Ryle, "Systematically Misleading Expressions," 189.

2. For a detailed criticism of Ryle's position and an argument that expressions involving fictional names are not systematically misleading at all, see Parsons, "Are There Nonexistent Objects?"

3. For a contemporary Fregean theory, see Künne, "Fictional Discourse."

4. Adding a clause such as "but there is a play such that according to the play, it does present a man" to the paraphrase might do better at yielding appropriate truth conditions, although it begins to become an implausibly contorted reading of a seemingly straightforward statement.

5. See, e.g., Parsons, "Fregean Theories"; Crittenden, *Unreality*, Chapters 1, 2.

6. Parsons, *Nonexistent Objects*, 36.

7. Walton, *Mimesis as Make-Believe*, 400.

8. Further criticisms of the pretense view, based on its inadequacy in handling real objects in fictional contexts, may be found in Kroon, "Make-Believe."

9. Walton, *Mimesis as Make-Believe*, 423.

10. For a discussion of Mally's solutions, see Zalta, *Abstract Objects*, 10–11.

11. Parsons, *Nonexistent Objects*, 23.

12. See *Nonexistent Objects*, 38–42. Those queasy about giving up such principles may find one of the other solutions more congenial.

13. Zalta, *Abstract Objects*, 13–14.

14. They may also encode some extranuclear properties (Zalta, *Abstract Objects*, 39).

15. Zalta, *Abstract Objects*, 10–13.

16. For Parsons, however, "creates" must not be taken in the sense of "brings into existence" or "makes them objects" but rather as "makes them *fictional*" (*Nonexistent Objects*, 188).

17. Zalta takes "create" in a similarly disarmed sense, presumably to designate the extranuclear relation of authoring (*Abstract Objects*, 91).

18. Parsons, *Nonexistent Objects*, 44.

19. Parsons, *Nonexistent Objects*, 51; Zalta, *Abstract Objects*, 95.

20. Parsons, *Nonexistent Objects*, 57–59.

21. In the context of Irvin D. Yalom's *When Nietzsche Wept*.

22. Lewis ("Truth in Fiction") also advocates the view that some, but not all, statements about fictional characters should be read as prefixed with a story operator, although he limits himself to analyzing statements of the implicitly prefixed variety.

23. See, for example, D. W. Smith's analysis in terms of the Husserlian notion of horizon ("Bounds of Fiction"), Lewis's analysis of prefixed statements in terms of possible worlds ("Truth in Fiction"), and Parsons's discussion in *Nonexistent Objects*, 175–182.

24. If we take the statements to occur in a real context, then the unprefixed statement "Hamlet is of bloodtype A" comes out as false, and "it is not the case that Hamlet is of bloodtype A" comes out as true, for he is a fictional character, after all – he has no blood. So from the real-world perspective we can say that Hamlet is not incomplete with respect to the property *being of bloodtype A*; he lacks the property.

25. Anyone who takes including the same set of propositions as a necessary condition for the identity of a story will treat all claims about properties possibly, but not actually, ascribed to a character by a story as false. On the other hand, if one treats stories as constructed objects with their most important identity conditions lying in the preservation of their origin and important items of content, one could allow that a story could ascribe to a character slightly different properties than it, in fact, does. On such a theory, certain B-type statements, like the trivial one about Watson, could be true (as this could be altered without the story losing its identity). But even so, the statement B would come out as false, as killing the Arab is the pivotal event of the story.

26. Walton, *Mimesis as Make-Believe*, 386.

27. Parsons, "Are There Nonexistent Objects?," 366.

CHAPTER 8

1. This distinction between the two tasks of ontology has been made frequently and in many different ways: Williams (*Principles of Empirical Realism*, 74) calls the first "analytic ontology" and the latter "speculative cosmology"; Ingarden (*Der Streit*, vol. I, 21–53) labels these tasks "ontology" and "metaphysics" respectively. See also discussion in the introduction to Hoffman and Rosenkrantz, *Substance among other Categories*.

2. Butchvarov ("Categories," 75) also mentions exhaustiveness and mutual exclusivity as the two essential conditions placed on an ideal set of categories.

3. Chisholm, *On Metaphysics* and *Realistic Theory of Categories*; Rosenkrantz and Hoffman, *Substance among other Categories*; Johansson, *Ontological Investigations*; Grossman, *Categorial Structure*.

4. Collingwood, *Essay on Metaphysics*; Körner, *Categorial Frameworks*.

5. Chisolm, *On Metaphysics*, 162 ff; Hoffman and Rosenkrantz, *Substance among other Categories*, 18 ff.

6. Hoffman and Rosenkrantz, *Substance among other Categories*, 20 (n. 27).

7. Butchvarov ("Categories," 76) mentions several other potential overlap problems with Aristotle's category scheme.

8. Hoffman and Rosenkrantz, *Substance among other Categories*, 20 (n. 27).

9. This terminology follows Ingarden's (*Der Streit*), who introduced the idea of an existential ontology alongside the formal and material ontologies of Husserl.

10. The type of dependence at issue in devising these categories is material dependence, although these also include formal dependencies, because formal dependence entails material dependence. Other charts could be drawn out to detail a thing's nomological dependencies (see Chapter 2 for these distinctions). The dependence usually claimed to hold between the mental and the physical is nomological and hence does not appear here. Taking the mental and real as fundaments does not presuppose a fundamental dualism or mutual independence between the mental and the physical; for present purposes the question of the relations between these two fundaments may simply be left open.

11. Thus by "real" I do *not* mean real in the sense of existent, as opposed to the unreal or nonexistent.

12. Reism such as that defended by Kotarbiński (*Elements*) provides an example of an ontology that rejects not only anything that is not a spatiotemporal individual, but also anything that is dependent on something else (for example, moments, events, and processes), accepting only particular things. For discussion see B. Smith, *Austrian Philosophy*, 193–242.

13. The many different meanings associated with "the abstract" have been noted before, for example by Hoffman and Rosenkrantz (*Substance among other Categories*; appendix); Lowe, ("Metaphysics of Abstract Objects").

14. Zalta's theory of abstract objects as eternal and necessary entities captures this use of "abstract" (*Abstract Objects*).

15. This is how it is defined, for example, by Jacquette ("Abstract Entity," in Audi, ed., *Cambridge Dictionary of Philosophy*).

16. Searle, *Construction of Social Reality*, 23–26.

17. Margolis, "Ontological Peculiarity," 257–258.

18. See, e.g., Searle, *Construction of Social Reality*; Smith and Zaibert, "Prolegomena."

19. Ingarden offers similar detailed analyses of the ontological status of literary works, especially arguing for their nonconcrete status (*Literary Work of Art*, 7–19), and of musical works (*Ontology*, 90–122).

20. Levinson, *Music, Art and Metaphysics*, 83. See also his argument that origin is essential to the identity of the musical work, 82–86.

21. Although this is, of course, precisely what many realist views of properties, be they Aristotelian or Platonist, traditionally claim. One could, of course, take the Platonist view that there has always been the form of the telephone, and hence the kind; or an *in rebus* universals view that claims that, provided there is a

164

telephone at some time, the kind *telephone* always existed. In both of these views all that changed is that there became examples of that kind after the "invention" of the telephone (which was really a discovery of that preexisting kind). But although one could take such a view, it seems far more natural to treat telephones, diesel engines, and the like to be genuinely new, invented kinds of things, and hence to take a constructivist view of them such as that described in the text. Although the debate about how to conceive of technological kinds cannot be settled here, such kinds should at least prove sufficient as examples of good candidates for entities generically historically dependent on certain activities.

22. A discussion of the inventors of the telephone may be found in Meyer, *Great Inventions*, 177–179.

23. Armstrong, *Universals*, 74–75.

24. Cf. Armstrong, *Universals*, 98–99.

25. Armstrong's example is being an Australian (*Universals*, 9).

CHAPTER 9

1. Linsky and Zalta ("Naturalized Platonism vs. Platonized Naturalism") coined the term "piecemeal Platonism" and argue against this approach.

2. Searle (*Construction of Social Reality*, Chapter 3) argues that language is required for the existence of *all* of the rest of institutional reality.

3. Nonetheless, a character need not be produced by a single author, certainly not in a single sitting. The creation process for fictional characters may vary greatly, not only by individual but also by culture and literary tradition, and the origin of a character may be diffuse, encompassing many different acts of many different people over a prolonged period of time (as is the case, for example, with many mythical heroes, and even with the Nancy Drew of our time). Yet however diffuse and hard to track the origin of a particular character may be, the same principle holds that the character must have originated from its particular origin, and none other.

4. This is true unless some argument is made that it is impossible to combine such characteristics. The definitions of these categories, however, give us no reason to think there should be any difficulty in combining these characteristics.

CHAPTER 10

1. Occasionally this problem *has* been noticed by those working with special problems such as the status of literary works, musical works, or artifacts, for example Ingarden, Levinson, and Hilpenin. Husserl's regional ontology, which includes a study of the region of *spirit* as well as those of *nature* and *consciousness*, also provides a detailed treatment of these intermediate dependent entities lying between the purely mental and purely material. See the second and third books of *Ideas* and a contemporary version in D. W. Smith, "Mind and Body."

2. This does not preclude that certain intentional states may depend mediately on forms of cultural practice, on language, or on context, as well as on brain events, provided that all of these, in turn, ultimately depend only on independent spatiotemporal entities.

Bibliography

Armstrong, David M. *Universals: An Opinionated Introduction.* Boulder, Colorado: Westview Press, 1989.
———. *A World of States of Affairs.* Cambridge: Cambridge University Press, 1997.
Audi, Robert, ed. *The Cambridge Dictionary of Philosophy.* Cambridge: Cambridge University Press, 1995.
Bach, Kent, and Robert M. Harnish. *Linguistic Communication and Speech Acts.* Cambridge, Massachusetts: MIT Press, 1979.
Benacerraf, Paul. "Mathematical Truth." *The Journal of Philosophy* LXX/19 (November 1973): 661–669.
Brennan, Andrew. *Conditions of Identity: A Study in Identity and Survival.* Oxford: Clarendon Press, 1988.
Butchvarov, Panayot. "Categories." In *A Companion to Metaphysics,* edited by Jaegwon Kim and Ernest Sosa. Oxford: Basil Blackwell, 1995.
Campbell, Keith. *Abstract Particulars.* Oxford: Blackwell, 1990.
Carr, Brian. *Metaphysics: An Introduction.* Atlantic Highlands, New Jersey: Humanities Press International, 1987.
Chisholm, Roderick. *On Metaphysics.* Minneapolis: University of Minnesota Press, 1989.
———. *A Realistic Theory of Categories.* Cambridge: Cambridge University Press, 1996.
Collingwood, R. G. *The Principles of Art.* New York: Oxford University Press, 1958.
———. *Essay on Metaphysics.* Oxford: Oxford University Press, 1940.
Crittenden, Charles. *Unreality: The Metaphysics of Fictional Objects.* Ithaca, New York: Cornell University Press, 1991.
Dodd, J. E. *The Ideas of Particle Physics.* Cambridge: Cambridge University Press, 1984.
Eliot, George. *Silas Marner.* New York: Bantam Classics Edition, 1981.
Evans, Gareth. *The Varieties of Reference.* Oxford: Clarendon Press, 1982.
Findlay, J. N. *Meinong's Theory of Objects and Values,* 2d edition. Oxford: Oxford University Press, 1963.
Fine, Kit. "Model Theory for Modal Logic Part 1." *Journal of Philosophical Logic* 7 (1978): 125–156.

————. "Ontological Dependence," *Proceedings of the Aristotelian Society*, vol. 95 (1995): 269–290.

Frege, Gottlob. "On Sense and Nominatum." In *The Philosophy of Language*, 2d ed., edited by A. P. Martinich. New York: Oxford University Press, 1990.

Gorman, Michael. "Logical and Metaphysical Form: Lessons from the Theory of Dependence." *Proceedings of the American Catholic Philosophical Association* LXIX (1995): 217–226.

Grossmann, Reinhardt. *The Categorial Structure of the World*. Bloomington: Indiana University Press, 1983.

Hilpinen, Risto. "Artifact." (Unpublished manuscript.)

————. "On Artifacts and Works of Art." *Theoria* 58 (1992): 58–82.

Hirsch, Eli. *The Concept of Identity*. Oxford: Oxford University Press, 1982.

Hoffman, Joshua, and Gary S. Rosenkrantz. *Substance among other Categories*. Cambridge: Cambridge University Press, 1994.

Hunter, Daniel. "Reference and Meinongian Objects." *Grazer Philosophische Studien* 14 (1981): 23–36.

Husserl, Edmund. *Ideas Pertaining to a Pure Phenomenology and to a Phenomenological Philosophy*, second book, translated by R. Rojcewicz and A. Schuwer. Dordrecht: Kluwer, 1989.

————. *Logical Investigations*, vol. 2, translated by J. N. Findlay. London: Routledge and Kegan Paul, 1970.

Ingarden, Roman. *The Literary Work of Art*, translated by George G. Grabowicz. Evanston, Illinois: Northwestern University Press, 1973.

————. *The Ontology of the Work of Art*, translated by Raymond Meyer. Athens, Ohio: Ohio University Press, 1989.

————. *Der Streit um die Existenz der Welt*, Tübingen: Max Niemeyer, 1965.

————. *Time and Modes of Being*, translated by Helen R. Michejda. Springfield, Illinois: Charles C. Thomas Publisher, 1964.

Jacquette, Dale. "Abstract Entity." In *Cambridge Dictionary of Philosophy*, edited by Robert Audi. New York: Cambridge University Press, 1995.

Johansson, Ingvar. *Ontological Investigations*. New York: Routledge, 1989.

Kim, Jaegwon. *Supervenience and Mind*. Cambridge: Cambridge University Press, 1993.

————. "Supervenience as a Philosophical Concept." *Metaphilosophy* 21, nos. 1 and 2 (1990): 1–27.

Kim, Jaegwon, and Ernest Sosa, eds. *A Companion to Metaphysics*. Cambridge, Massachusetts: Blackwell, 1995.

Körner, Stephan. *Categorial Frameworks*. Oxford: Basil Blackwell, 1974.

Kotarbińsky, Tadeusz. *Elements of the Theory of Knowledge*, translated by O. Wojtasiewicz in *Gnosiology: The Scientific Approach to the Theory of Knowledge*. Oxford: Pergamon, 1966.

Kripke, Saul. *Naming and Necessity*. Cambridge, Massachusetts: Harvard University Press, 1972.

————. "Semantical Considerations on Modal Logic." In *Reference and Modality*, edited by Leonard Linsky. Oxford: Oxford University Press, 1971.

Kroon, Frederick. "Make-Believe and Fictional Reference." *Journal of Aesthetics and Art Criticism* 52, no. 2 (1994): 207–214.

————. "A Problem about Make-Belief." *Philosophical Studies* 73, no. 3 (1994): 201–229.

————. "Was Meinong only Pretending?" *Philosophy and Phenomenological Research* 52, no. 3 (1992): 499–527.

Künne, Wolfgang. "Fictional Discourse without Fictitious Objects: Towards a Fregean Theory of Fiction." Unpublished manuscript presented at the University of Venice, June 1993.

Lambert, Karel. *Meinong and the Principle of Independence.* Cambridge: Cambridge University Press, 1983.

Lambert, Karel, ed. *Philosophical Applications of Free Logic.* New York: Oxford University Press, 1991.

Levinson, Jerrold. *Music, Art and Metaphysics.* Ithaca, New York: Cornell University Press, 1990.

Lewis, David. *On the Plurality of Worlds.* Oxford: Blackwell Publishers, 1986.

————. "Truth in Fiction." *American Philosophical Quarterly* 15, no. 1 (1978): 37–46.

Linsky, Bernard, and Edward N. Zalta. "Naturalized Platonism vs. Platonized Naturalism." *The Journal of Philosophy* XCII, no. 10 (1995): 525–555.

Lowe, E. J. "The Metaphysics of Abstract Objects." *The Journal of Philosophy* XCII, no. 10 (1995): 509–524.

Margolis, Joseph. "The Ontological Peculiarity of Works of Art," in *Philosophy Looks at the Arts*, 3d edition. Philadelphia: Temple University Press, 1987.

Meinong, Alexius. "On the Theory of Objects." In *Realism and the Background of Phenomenology*, edited by Roderick Chisholm. Atascadero, California: Ridgeview, 1960.

————. *Über Möglichkeit und Wahrscheinlichkeit.* In *Alexius Meinong Gesamtausgabe*, volume VI, edited by Roderick Chisholm. Graz, Austria: Akademische Druck u. Verlagsanstalt, 1972.

Meyer, Jerome S. *Great Inventions.* New York: Pocketbooks, 1962.

Moore, G. E. *Lectures on Philosophy*, edited by Casimir Lewy. London: George Allen & Unwin, 1966.

Parsons, Terence. "Are there Nonexistent Objects?" *American Philosophical Quarterly* 19, no. 4 (1982): 365–371.

————. "Entities without Identity." In *Philosophical Perspective 1: Metaphysics*, edited by James E. Tomberlin. Atascadero, California: Ridgeview, 1987.

————. "Fregean Theories of Fictional Objects." *Topoi* 1 (1982): 81–87.

————. *Nonexistent Objects.* New Haven: Yale University Press, 1980.

Plantinga, Alvin. *The Nature of Necessity.* Oxford: Clarendon Press, 1974.

Posy, Carl J. "Brouwer's Constructivism." *Synthese* 27 (1974): 125–159.

Putnam, Hilary. *Reason, Truth and History.* Cambridge: Cambridge University Press, 1981.

Quine, W. V. O. "On What There Is." In *From a Logical Point of View*. Cambridge, Massachusetts: Harvard University Press, 1953.

Quine, W. V. O., and Nelson Goodman. "Steps Toward a Constructive Nominalism." *Journal of Symbolic Logic* 12 (1947): 105–122.

Rapaport, William J. "Meinongian Theories and a Russellian Paradox." *Nous* 12 (1978): 153–180.

Reicher, Maria. "Zur Identität fiktiver Gegenstände: Ein Kommentar zu Amie Thomasson." *Conceptus* XXVIII (1995), no. 72: 93–116.

Russell, Bertrand. "On Denoting." In *The Philosophy of Language*, edited by A. P. Martinich, 2d edition. New York: Oxford University Press, 1990.

Ryle, Gilbert. "Systematically Misleading Expressions." Reprinted in *Twentieth-Century Philosophy: The Analytic Tradition*, edited by Morris Weitz. New York: The Free Press, 1966.

Sajama, Seppo, and Matti Kamppinen. A *Historical Introduction to Phenomenology*. New York: Croom Helm, 1987.

Salmon, Nathan. *Reference and Essence*. Princeton, New Jersey: Princeton University Press, 1981.

Sartre, Jean Paul. *The Psychology of Imagination*. New York: Carol Publishing Group, 1991.

Searle, John. *The Construction of Social Reality*. New York: The Free Press, 1995.

———. *Intentionality*. New York: Cambridge University Press, 1983.

Simons, Peter. *Parts*. New York: Oxford University Press, 1987.

———. *Philosophy and Logic in Central Europe from Bolzano to Tarski*. Dordrecht, The Netherlands: Kluwer, 1992.

Smith, Barry. *Austrian Philosophy*. Chicago: Open Court, 1994.

———. "Historicity, Value and Mathematics." *Analecta Husserliana* 4 (1975): 219–39.

———. "Ingarden vs. Meinong on the Logic of Fiction." *Philosophy and Phenomenological Research* 16 (1980): 93–105.

———, ed. *Parts and Moments*. Munich: Philosophia, 1982.

Smith, Barry, and Hans Burkhardt, eds. *Handbook of Metaphysics and Ontology*. Munich: Philosophia, 1991.

Smith, Barry, and David Woodruff Smith, eds. *The Cambridge Companion to Husserl*. Cambridge: Cambridge University Press, 1995.

Smith, Barry, and Leonardo Zaibert. "Prolegomena to a Metaphysics of Real Estate." (Unpublished manuscript.)

Smith, David Woodruff. "The Background of Intentionality." (Unpublished manuscript.)

———. "The Bounds of Fiction." (Unpublished manuscript.)

———. *The Circle of Acquaintance*. Dordrecht: Kluwer Academic Publishers, 1989.

———. "Meinongian Objects." *Grazer Philosophische Studien* 1 (1975): 43–71.

———. "Mind and Body." In *The Cambridge Companion to Husserl*, edited by Barry Smith and David Woodruff Smith. Cambridge: Cambridge University Press, 1995.

———. "Thoughts." *Philosophical Papers* XIX, no. 3 (1990): 163–189.

Smith, David Woodruff, and Ronald McIntyre. *Husserl and Intentionality*. Dordrecht: D. Reidel Publishing Co., 1982.

Thomasson, Amie L. "Fiction and Intentionality." *Philosophy and Phenomenological Research* 56 (June 1996): 277–298.

———. "Fiction, Modality and Dependent Abstracta." *Philosophical Studies* 84, nos. 2–3 (1996): 295–320.

———. "Fictional Characters: Dependent or Abstract? A Reply to Reicher's Objections." *Conceptus* XXIX, no. 74 (1996): 119–144.

————."Die Identität fiktionaler Gegenstände." *Conceptus* XXVII, no. 70 (1994): 77–95.

————. "Ingarden and the Theory of Dependence." (Unpublished manuscript.)

————. "The Ontology of the Social World in Searle, Husserl and Beyond." *Phenomenological Inquiry* 21, in press.

Twardowski, Kasimir. *On the Content and Object of Presentations*, translated by R. Grossmann. The Hague: Martinus Nijhoff, 1977.

van Inwagen, Peter. "Creatures of Fiction." *American Philosophical Quarterly* 14, no. 4 (1977): 299–308.

————. "Fiction and Metaphysics." *Philosophy and Literature* 7 (1983): 67–77.

Walton, Kendall. *Mimesis as Make-Believe*. Cambridge, Massachusetts: Harvard University Press, 1990.

Wiggins, David. *Identity and Spatio-Temporal Continuity*. Oxford: Blackwell, 1967.

Williams, Donald Cary. *Principles of Empirical Realism*. Springfield, Illinois: Charles C. Thomas, 1966.

Wollheim, Richard. *Art and Its Objects*. New York: Harper and Row, 1968.

Wolterstorff, Nicholas. *Works and Worlds of Art*. Oxford: Clarendon Press, 1980.

Woods, John. *The Logic of Fiction*. The Hague: Mouton and Co., 1974.

Yalom, Irvin D. *When Nietzsche Wept*. New York: Basic Books, 1992.

Zalta, Edward. *Abstract Objects*. The Netherlands: Reidel, 1983.

————. *Intensional Logic and the Metaphysics of Intentionality*. Cambridge, Massachusetts: Massachusetts Institute of Technology Press, 1988.

————. "Referring to Fictional Characters." (Unpublished manuscript. A version translated into German appears in *Zeitschrift für Semiotik* 9 nos. 1–2 (1987): 85–95.)

170

Index

abstract artifacts, *see* artifacts, abstract
abstracta
  defined, 126–7
  dependent, 37–8, 40–2, 131–4,
    see also artifacts, abstract
  independent, 37–8, 40–1, 125–7,
    135, 151, *see also* ideal entities
  in modal metaphysics, 40–2
  reference to, 44, 52–4
Andrews, Pamela, 7, 56–7, 66, 68,
  83–4, 90–1
Animal Farm, 8–9
Armstrong, David, 130–1, 133–4,
  158n5 (41)
art, works of
  dependence on mental states, 13,
    129–30
  dependence on real entities, 131–2
  fall between traditional, categories,
    135, 148–9
  similarities to fictional characters,
    144, 146
artifacts
  abstract, xii, 37–8, 40–2, 126, 148–9,
    153
  creation of, 12–14, 27
  dependence on mental states, 129–30
  fall between traditional categories,
    148–9
  fictional characters as, xi–xii, 10, 14,
    35–8, 73, 139–40, 147

literary works as, 9–10
place in an adequate ontology, 151–3
see also cultural objects; social objects
artifactual theory
  of character identity, 63–9
  contrasted with other theories of
    fiction, 14–23
  of fictional characters, 3, 5–14,
    35–40, 139–43
  of fictional discourse, 105–14
  of reference to fictional characters,
    46–52
authors
  dependence of fictional characters on,
    5–7, 35, 39, 140, 142
  dependence of literary works on,
    8–9, 141, 142
  as genuine creators, 5–6, 12, 15–16,
    40
  role in character identity across texts,
    67–8
  role in naming characters, 47–8

baptism of fictional characters, 46–9

cars, models of, 52–3, 126, 159n12
categories
  between the material and the mental,
    128–31
  between the real and the ideal, 131–4
  criteria of adequacy for, 117

171

categories (*cont.*)
  inadequacies of traditional, xii, 118–20, 126–8, 135–6, 148–9
  location of familiar, 124–7
  skepticism about, 117–20
  system of existential, 120–34
  traditional systems of, 118–9
  uses of, 115–7, 134–6
chains of communication and publication, 49–52
Chisholm, Roderick, 118–9
Collingwood, R. G., 118
composition, 64–6
conception dependence, 77–8, 79–83, 88, 90
concreta, 126–7, 134
constructivism, 41, 119, 135
content theory, 76–84
context sensitivity, 77–8, 83–4, 90–1
conventional illocutionary acts, 12–13
copy, 64–5
creation of fictional characters, 5–7, 12–13
Crittenden, Charles, 18–21
cultural objects
  dependencies of, 128–30, 132–3
  place in an adequate ontology, 149–50, 151–3
  similarities to fictional characters, xi–xii, 12–14, 55, 73, 146–7
  see also art, works of; artifacts; music, works of; social objects

dependence
  constant, 29, 30–1
  general, 25, 29–30
  generic, 27
  historical, 29, 31–3
  need for a general theory of, 24–7
  prior studies of, 24–6
  relations among kinds of, 33–4, 122–3
  rigid, 27
  self-, 26
  variations in, 27–9
dependent abstracta, *see* abstracta, dependent

eliminative materialism, 121–2
encoding/exemplifying distinction, 15, 101–2
essential part, 30
essential property, 31
Evans, Gareth, 44, 50
everyday world,
  ontology for, 150–3
  relevance of fictional characters for understanding, xi–xii, 14, 24, 35–6, 146–7
  unaccounted for in traditional ontologies, 148–50
exhaustiveness of category systems, 117, 118–9, 122, 127
experience of fictional characters (*see also* intentionality), 76–92
  importance to theories of intentionality, 78–9, 92
  motivates postulating fictional characters, 73–5, 92, 147

Faust, 58–60
fictional characters
  as abstract artifacts, xi–xii, 35–8, 73, 139–40, 147
  baptism of, 46–9
  categorization of, 139–43
  characteristics of, 5–12
  creation of, 5–7, 12–13
  dependencies of, 24, 35–6, 140–3
  destruction of, 10–11
  as imaginary objects, 21–2
  maintenance of, 7–12, 23
  as Meinongian objects, *see* Meinongian theories
  in modal metaphysics, 38–40
  as objects of reference, 18–21
  reference to, 43–4, 46–52
  similar to other cultural entities, 12–14, 144, 146–7, 148–9
  whether we should postulate, 3–4, 73–5, 92, 113–4, 147–50
fictional discourse, 74, 93–114, 147
  artifactual theory of, 105–14
  in fictional contexts, 94–5, 97, 100–2, 105–11, 113

material entities, 124–5, 128, 131,
     148–9
material necessity, 27–8
mathematical entities, 37–8, 41, 131,
     135, 151
  see also numbers
mediated relation, 89–90
Meinong, Alexius, 14–17, 89–90
Meinongian theories
  of fictional characters, 14–17, 18,
     38–40,
  of fictional discourse, 100–5, 107, 113
  identity conditions in, 56–62
  of intentionality, 76–7
mental states, 121, 125, 129
  categories of dependence on, 124–5,
     128–31, 134, 150–3
  dependence of fictional characters on,
     142–3
metaphysics (*see also* ontology)
  modal, 38–42
  relevance of fiction to, xi–xii
money, 13–14, 23, 128, 130, 134
music, works of, 41, 131–2, 134, 148,
     152
  reference to, 53–4

names, causal theory of, 43–6, 52–4
names, fictional, 43–52, 54
  applied in baptism, 46–9
  Kripke on, 44–6
  passed on in chains of reference,
     49–52
necessity, strengths of, 27–8, 164n10.
Nixon, Richard, 9, 37, 104–5
nomological necessity, 27–8, 152
nonexistence claims, 112–3
nonexistent objects, 14–17, 100–3
  see also Meinongian theories
nonreferring terms, 43–6, 93–6
nuclear/extra-nuclear distinction, 15,
     100
numbers, 125, 134, 144–5
  see also mathematical entities

Ockham's razor, 116–7, 138
  see also parsimony

ontology
  categorial, 116–7
  method for making decisions about,
     3–4, 73–5, 115–7, 136
  piecemeal, 115–7, 144–5
  proposal for an adequate, 150–3
  two tasks of, 115–6

paraphrase, 94–7, 99–100, 104–5,
     107–8, 112–3
parsimony, 74–5, 115–7, 137–45,
     147–8, 153
  genuine versus false, 137–9, 143–5
  not gained merely by rejecting
     fictional characters, 143–5
Parsons, Terence, 14–17, 56–7, 96,
     100–1, 102–5, 112, 161n17
Plantinga, Alvin, 17–18
possibilia, 17–18, 38, 40, 44–5
possible fictional characters, 40
possible worlds, 38–42
pretense theories, 97–100
properties
  in dependence relations, 26–7, 30–1,
     32, 34
  as means of identifying fictional
     characters, 56–62
  see also universals
purely intentional objects, 22–3, 89

Quine, W. V. O., 55

readers
  capabilities and background
     assumptions required of, 65–6,
     159n9
  dependence on, 11–12, 139–40,
     142–3
  role in naming practices, 49–50
real entities, 121, 125–6
  as basis for an adequate ontology,
     150–3
  categories of dependence on, 131–4
real people in fictional contexts, 104–5,
     106–7, 108
reference to fictional characters, 43–4,
     46–52

174

reference shifts, 51–2, 68–9
Reicher, Maria, 61–2
Rosenkrantz, Gary, 118–9
Russell, Bertrand, 55, 94–5
Ryle, Gilbert, 95

Sartre, Jean Paul, 21–3, 135
Searle, John, 12–14, 76–7, 128
sequels, 61–2, 67–8
Smith, David Woodruff, 76–8, 81–2
social objects, 12–14, 128–30, 135,
     149–53
   see also artifacts; cultural objects;
     money
spatiotemporal entities, *see* real entities
states of affairs, 26–7, 30–1, 33, 34

telephone, 133, 164–5n21
text, 64–5
tropes, 26–7
Twardowski, Kasimir, 162n16
"twin" characters, 56–7, 66, 68, 83–4,
     90–91

universals, 29, 41, 130–1, 133–4

van Inwagen, Peter, 18, 20–21

Walton, Kendall, 97–9, 112
Wolterstorff, Nicholas, 58–60

Zalta, Edward, 14–17, 56–7, 101–5,
     159n8, 162n16

977186

Printed in Great Britain by
Amazon.co.uk, Ltd.,
Marston Gate.